General Explanations
of the
Administration's Fiscal Year 2012
Revenue Proposals

Department of the Treasury
February 2011

TABLE OF CONTENTS[1]

---

[1] The Administration's policy proposals reflect changes from a tax baseline that modifies the Budget Enforcement Act baseline by permanently extending alternative minimum tax relief, freezing the estate tax at 2009 levels, and making permanent a number of the tax cuts enacted in 2001 and 2003. These baseline changes are described in the modified PAYGO baseline section.

TAX CUTS FOR FAMILIES AND INDIVIDUALS

PROVIDE $250 REFUNDABLE TAX CREDIT FOR FEDERAL, STATE AND LOCAL GOVERNMENT RETIREES NOT ELIGIBLE FOR SOCIAL SECURITY

Current Law

The American Recovery and Reinvestment Act of 2009 (ARRA) provided a one-time $250 payment for certain retirees and a $250 refundable tax credit for recipients of government pensions who were not eligible for the $250 payments.

Economic Recovery Payments: A $250 Economic Recovery Payment was made in 2009 to each adult who was eligible ($500 to a married couple filing jointly where both spouses were eligible) for Social Security benefits, Railroad Retirement benefits, veterans benefits, or Supplemental Security Income (SSI) benefits (excluding individuals who receive SSI while in a Medicaid institution). Only individuals eligible to receive at least one of these benefits in the three-month period prior to February 2009 were eligible for an Economic Recovery Payment. Individuals received only one Economic Recovery Payment even if they were eligible for more than one type of benefit.

Special Tax Credit for Certain Government Retirees: Federal, State and local government retirees who received a pension or annuity from work not covered by Social Security and who were not eligible to receive an Economic Recovery Payment were entitled to claim a $250 refundable income tax credit ($500 for a married couple filing jointly where both spouses were eligible) for 2009.

Reasons for Change

Another Administration proposal would provide a $250 special payment in 2011 to each adult who is eligible ($500 to a married couple filing jointly where both spouses are eligible) for Social Security benefits, Railroad Retirement benefits, veterans benefits, or Supplemental Security Income (SSI) benefits (excluding individuals who receive SSI while in a Medicaid institution). The special tax credit is intended to provide similar economic assistance to Federal, State and local government workers who are not eligible for Social Security benefits and who are not eligible to receive the $250 special payment.

Proposal

The proposal would provide a $250 refundable tax credit in 2011 to Federal, State, and local government retirees who are not eligible for Social Security benefits and who are not eligible to receive the $250 special payment ($500 for a married couple filing jointly where both spouses would be eligible for the credit).

The proposal would be effective as of the date of enactment.

EXTEND THE EARNED INCOME TAX CREDIT (EITC) FOR LARGER FAMILIES

Current Law

Low and moderate-income workers may be eligible for a refundable EITC. Eligibility for the EITC is based on the presence and number of qualifying children in the worker's household, adjusted gross income (AGI), earned income, investment income, filing status, age, and immigration and work status in the United States. The amount of the EITC is based on the presence and number of qualifying children in the worker's household, AGI, earned income, and filing status.

The EITC has a phase-in range (where each additional dollar of earned income results in a larger credit), a maximum range (where additional dollars of earned income or AGI have no effect on the size of the credit), and a phase-out range (where each additional dollar of the larger of earned income or AGI results in a smaller total credit). The EITC for childless workers is much smaller and phases out at a lower income level than does the EITC for workers with qualifying children.

The EITC generally phases in at a faster rate for workers with more qualifying children, resulting in a larger maximum credit and a longer phase-out range. Prior to the enactment of the American Recovery and Reinvestment Act (ARRA), the credit reached its maximum at two or more qualifying children. ARRA increased the phase-in rate for families with three or more qualifying children through 2010. The Tax Relief, Unemployment Insurance Reauthorization and Job Creation Act of 2010 extended this provision through 2012. After 2012, workers with three or more qualifying children will receive the same EITC as similarly situated workers with two qualifying children.

The phase-out range for joint filers begins at a higher income level than for an individual with the same number of qualifying children who files as a single filer or as a head of household. The width of the phase-in range and the beginning of the phase-out range are indexed for inflation. Hence, the maximum amount of the credit and the end of the phase-out range are effectively indexed. The following chart summarizes the EITC parameters for 2011.

	Childless Taxpayers	Taxpayers with Qualifying Children		
		One Child	Two Children	Three or More
Phase-in rate	7.65%	34.00%	40.00%	45.00%
Minimum earnings for maximum credit	$6,070	$9,100	$12,780	$12,780
Maximum credit	$464	$3,094	$5,112	$5,751
Phase-out rate	7.65%	15.98%	21.06%	21.06%
Phase-out begins	$7,590 ($12,670 joint)	$16,690 ($21,770 joint)	$16,690 ($21,770 joint)	$16,690 ($21,770 joint)
Phase-out ends	$13,660 ($18,740 joint)	$36,052 ($41,132 joint)	$40,964 ($46,044 joint)	$43,998 ($49,078 joint)

To be eligible for the EITC, workers must have no more than $3,150 of investment income. (This amount is indexed for inflation.)

Reasons for Change

Families with more children face larger expenses related to raising their children than families with fewer children and as a result tend to have higher poverty rates. The steeper phase-in rate and larger maximum credit for workers with three or more qualifying children helps workers with larger families meet their expenses while maintaining work incentives.

Proposal

The proposal would make permanent the expansion of the EITC for workers with three or more qualifying children. Specifically, the phase-in rate of the EITC for workers with three or more qualifying children would be maintained at 45 percent, resulting in a higher maximum credit amount and a longer phase-out range.

The proposal would be effective for taxable years beginning after December 31, 2012.

EXPAND THE CHILD AND DEPENDENT CARE TAX CREDIT

Current Law

In 2011, taxpayers with child or dependent care expenses who are working or looking for work are eligible for a nonrefundable tax credit that partially offsets these expenses. Married couples are eligible only if they file a joint return and either both spouses are working or looking for work, or if one spouse is working or looking for work and the other is attending school full-time. To qualify for this benefit, the child and dependent care expenses must be for either (1) a child under age thirteen when the care was provided or (2) a disabled dependent of any age with the same place of abode as the taxpayer. Any allowable credit is reduced by the aggregate amount excluded from income under an employer-provided dependent care assistance program.

Eligible taxpayers may claim the credit for up to 35 percent of up to $3,000 in eligible expenses for one child or dependent and up to $6,000 in eligible expenses for more than one child or dependent. The percentage of expenses for which a credit may be taken decreases by 1 percentage point for every $2,000 (or part thereof) of adjusted gross income (AGI) over $15,000 until the percentage of expenses reaches 20 percent (at incomes above $43,000). There are no further income limits. The phase-down point and the amount of expenses eligible for the credit are not indexed for inflation.

Reasons for Change

Access to affordable child care is a barrier to employment or further schooling for some individuals. Assistance to individuals with child and dependent care expenses increases the ability of individuals to participate in the labor force or in education programs.

Proposal

The proposal would permanently increase from $15,000 to $75,000 the AGI level at which the credit begins to phase down. The percentage of expenses for which a credit may be taken would decrease at a rate of 1 percentage point for every $2,000 (or part thereof) of AGI over $75,000 until the percentage reached 20 percent (at incomes above $103,000). As under current law, there would be no further income limits and the phase-down point and the amount of expenses eligible for the credit would not be indexed for inflation.

The proposal would be effective for taxable years beginning after December 31, 2011.

PROVIDE FOR AUTOMATIC ENROLLMENT IN INDIVIDUAL RETIREMENT ACCOUNTS OR ANNUITIES (IRAS) AND DOUBLE THE TAX CREDIT FOR SMALL EMPLOYER PLAN STARTUP COSTS

Current Law

A number of tax-preferred, employer-sponsored retirement savings programs exist under current law. These include section 401(k) cash or deferred arrangements, section 403(b) programs for public schools and charitable organizations, section 457 plans for governments and nonprofit organizations, and simplified employee pensions (SEPs) and SIMPLE plans for small employers.

Small employers (those with no more than 100 employees) that adopt a new qualified retirement, SEP or SIMPLE plan are entitled to a temporary business tax credit equal to 50 percent of the employer's plan "startup costs," which are the expenses of establishing or administering the plan, including expenses of retirement-related employee education with respect to the plan. The credit is limited to a maximum of $500 per year for three years.

Individuals who do not have access to an employer-sponsored retirement savings arrangement may be eligible to make smaller tax-favored contributions to IRAs.

In 2011, IRA contributions are limited to $5,000 a year (plus $1,000 for those age 50 or older). Section 401(k) plans permit contributions (employee plus employer contributions) of up to $49,000 a year (of which $16,500 can be pre-tax employee contributions) plus $5,500 of additional pre-tax employee contributions for those age 50 or older.

Reasons for Change

For many years, until the recent economic downturn, the personal saving rate in the United States has been exceedingly low, and tens of millions of U.S. households have not placed themselves on a path to become financially prepared for retirement. In addition, the proportion of U.S. workers participating in employer-sponsored plans has remained stagnant for decades at no more than about half the total work force, notwithstanding repeated private- and public-sector efforts to expand coverage. Among employees eligible to participate in an employer-sponsored retirement savings plan such as a 401(k) plan, participation rates typically have ranged from two-thirds to three-quarters of eligible employees, but making saving easier by making it automatic has been shown to be remarkably effective at boosting participation.

Beginning in 1998, Treasury and the Internal Revenue Service (IRS) issued a series of rulings and other guidance (most recently in September 2009) defining, permitting, and encouraging automatic enrollment in 401(k) and other plans (i.e., enrolling employees by default unless they opt out). Automatic enrollment was further facilitated by the Pension Protection Act of 2006. In 401(k) plans, automatic enrollment has tended to increase participation rates to more than nine out of ten eligible employees. In contrast, for workers who lack access to a retirement plan at their workplace and are eligible to engage in tax-favored retirement saving by taking the initiative and making the decisions required to establish and contribute to an IRA, the IRA participation rate tends to be less than one out of ten.

Numerous employers, especially those with smaller or lower-wage work forces, have been reluctant to adopt a retirement plan for their employees, in part out of concern about their ability to afford the cost of making employer contributions or the per-capita cost of complying with tax-qualification and ERISA (Employee Retirement Income Security Act) requirements. These employers could help their employees save -- without employer contributions or plan qualification or ERISA compliance -- simply by making their payroll systems available as a conduit for regularly transmitting employee contributions to an employee's IRA. Such "payroll deduction IRAs" could build on the success of workplace-based payroll-deduction saving by using the capacity to promote saving that is inherent in employer payroll systems, and the effort to help employees save would be especially effective if automatic enrollment were used. However, despite efforts more than a decade ago by the Department of the Treasury, the IRS, and the Department of Labor to approve and promote the option of payroll deduction IRAs, few employers have adopted them or even are aware that this option exists.

Accordingly, requiring employers that do not sponsor any retirement plan (and meet other criteria such as being above a certain size) to make their payroll systems available to employees and automatically enroll them in IRAs could achieve a major breakthrough in retirement savings coverage. In addition, requiring automatic IRAs may lead many employers to take the next step and adopt an employer plan, thereby permitting much greater tax-favored employee contributions than an IRA, plus the option of employer contributions. The potential for the use of automatic IRAs to lead to the adoption of 401(k) s, SIMPLEs, and other employer plans would be enhanced by raising the existing small employer tax credit for the startup costs of adopting a new retirement plan to an amount significantly higher than both its current level and the level of the proposed new automatic IRA tax credit for employers.

In addition, the process of saving and choosing investments in automatic IRAs could be simplified for employees, and costs minimized, through a standard default investment as well as electronic information and fund transfers. Workplace retirement savings arrangements made accessible to most workers also could be used as a platform to provide and promote retirement distributions over the worker's lifetime.

Proposal

The proposal would require employers in business for at least two years that have more than ten employees to offer an automatic IRA option to employees, under which regular contributions would be made to an IRA on a payroll-deduction basis. If the employer sponsored a qualified retirement plan, SEP, or SIMPLE for its employees, it would not be required to provide an automatic IRA option for its employees. Thus, for example, a qualified plan sponsor would not have to offer automatic IRAs to employees it excludes from qualified plan eligibility because they are covered by a collective bargaining agreement, under age eighteen, nonresident aliens, or have not completed the plan's eligibility waiting period. However, if the qualified plan excluded from eligibility a portion of the employer's work force or a class of employees such as all employees of a subsidiary or division, the employer would be required to offer the automatic IRA option to those excluded employees.

The employer offering automatic IRAs would give employees a standard notice and election form informing them of the automatic IRA option and allowing them to elect to participate or opt out. Any employee who did not provide a written participation election would be enrolled at a default rate of three percent of the employee's compensation in an IRA. Employees could opt out or opt for a lower or higher contribution rate up to the IRA dollar limits. Employees could choose either a traditional IRA or a Roth IRA, with Roth being the default. For most employees, the payroll deductions would be made by direct deposit similar to the direct deposit of employees' paychecks to their accounts at financial institutions.

Payroll-deduction contributions from all participating employees could be transferred, at the employer's option, to a single private-sector IRA trustee or custodian designated by the employer. Alternatively, the employer, if it preferred, could allow each participating employee to designate the IRA provider for that employee's contributions or could designate that all contributions would be forwarded to a savings vehicle specified by statute or regulation.

Employers making payroll deduction IRAs available would not have to choose or arrange default investments. Instead, a low-cost, standard type of default investment and a handful of standard, low-cost investment alternatives would be prescribed by statute or regulation. In addition, this approach would involve no employer contributions, no employer compliance with qualified plan requirements, and no employer liability or responsibility for determining employee eligibility to make tax-favored IRA contributions or for opening IRAs for employees. A national web site would provide information and basic educational material regarding saving and investing for retirement, including IRA eligibility, but, as under current law, individuals (not employers) would bear ultimate responsibility for determining their IRA eligibility.

Contributions by employees to automatic IRAs would qualify for the saver's credit to the extent the contributor and the contributions otherwise qualified.

Employers could claim a temporary tax credit for making automatic payroll-deposit IRAs available to employees. The amount of the credit for a year would be $25 per enrolled employee up to $250, and the credit would be available for two years. The credit would be available both to employers required to offer automatic IRAs and employers not required to do so (for example, because they have ten or fewer employees).

In conjunction with the automatic IRA proposal, to encourage employers not currently sponsoring a qualified retirement plan, SEP, or SIMPLE to do so, the "startup costs" tax credit for a small employer that adopts a new qualified retirement, SEP, or SIMPLE plan would be doubled from the current maximum of $500 per year for three years to a maximum of $1,000 per year for three years. This expanded "startup costs" credit for small employers, like the current "startup costs" credit, would not apply to automatic or other payroll deduction IRAs. The expanded credit would encourage small employers that would otherwise adopt an automatic IRA to adopt a new 401(k), SIMPLE, or other employer plan instead, while also encouraging other small employers to adopt a new employer plan.

The proposal would become effective after December 31, 2012.

EXTEND THE AMERICAN OPPORTUNITY TAX CREDIT (AOTC)

Current Law

Prior to enactment of the American Recovery and Reinvestment Act of 2009 (ARRA) an individual taxpayer could claim a nonrefundable Hope Scholarship credit for 100 percent of the first $1,200 and 50 percent of the next $1,200 in qualified tuition and related expenses (for a maximum credit of $1,800) per student. The Hope Scholarship credit was available only for the first two years of postsecondary education.

Alternatively, a taxpayer could claim a nonrefundable Lifetime Learning Credit (LLC) for 20 percent of up to $10,000 in qualified tuition and related expenses (for a maximum credit of $2,000) per taxpayer. Both the Hope Scholarship credit and LLC were phased out in 2009 between $50,000 and $60,000 of adjusted gross income ($100,000 and $120,000 if married filing jointly). In addition, through 2009, a taxpayer could claim an above-the-line deduction for qualified tuition and related expenses. The maximum amount of the deduction was $4,000.

ARRA created the AOTC to replace the Hope Scholarship credit for taxable years 2009 and 2010. The Tax Relief, Unemployment Reauthorization and Job Creation Act of 2010 extended the AOTC to taxable years 2011 and 2012. The AOTC is partially refundable, has a higher maximum credit amount, is available for the first four years of postsecondary education, and has higher income phase-out limits.

The AOTC equals 100 percent of the first $2,000, plus 25 percent of the next $2,000, of qualified tuition and related expenses (for a maximum credit of $2,500). For the AOTC, the definition of related expenses was expanded to include course materials. Forty percent of the otherwise allowable AOTC is refundable (for a maximum refundable credit of $1,000). The credit is available for the first four years of postsecondary education. The credit phases out for taxpayers with adjusted gross income between $80,000 and $90,000 ($160,000 and $180,000 if married filing jointly).

All other aspects of the Hope Scholarship credit are retained under the AOTC. These include the requirement that AOTC recipients be enrolled at least half-time.

Reasons for Change

The AOTC makes college more affordable for millions of middle-income families and for the first time makes college tax incentives partially refundable. If college is not made more affordable, our nation runs the risk of losing a whole generation of potential and productivity.

Making the AOTC partially refundable increases the likelihood that low-income families will send their children to college. Under prior law, low-income families (those without sufficient income tax liability) could not benefit from the Hope Scholarship credit or the Lifetime Learning Credit because they were not refundable. Under the proposal, low-income families could benefit from the refundable portion of the AOTC. The maximum available credit in 2011 would cover about 80 percent of tuition and fees at the average 2-year public institution, or about a third of tuition and fees at the average four-year public institution in 2011.

Moreover, the AOTC is available for the first four years of college, instead of only the first two years of college, increasing the likelihood that students will stay in school and attain their degrees. More years of schooling translates into higher future incomes (on average) for students and a more educated workforce for the country.

Finally, the higher phase-out thresholds under the AOTC give targeted tax relief to an even greater number of middle-income families facing the high costs of college.

Proposal

The proposal would make the AOTC a permanent replacement for the Hope Scholarship credit. To preserve the value of the AOTC, the proposal would index the $2,000 tuition and expense amounts, as well as the phase-out thresholds, for inflation.

This proposal would be effective for taxable years beginning after December 31, 2012.

PROVIDE EXCLUSION FROM INCOME FOR CERTAIN STUDENT LOAN FORGIVENESS

Current Law

In general, loan amounts that are forgiven are considered gross income to the borrower and subject to individual income tax in the year of discharge. Exceptions exist for certain student loan repayment programs. Specifically, students who participate in the National Health Service Corps Loan Repayment program, certain state loan repayment programs, and certain profession-based loans may exclude discharged amounts from gross income.

Students with higher education expenses may be eligible to borrow money for their education through the Federal Direct Loan Program. Prior to July 1, 2010, they may also have been eligible to borrow money through the Federal Family Education Loan Program. Both programs are administered by the Department of Education. Each program provides borrowers with an option for repaying the loan this is related to the borrower's income level after college (the income-contingent and the income-based repayment options). Under both of these options borrowers complete their repayment obligation when they have repaid the loan in full, with interest, or have made those payments that are required under the plan for 25 years. For those who reach the 25-year point, any remaining loan balance is forgiven. Under current law, any debt forgiven by these programs is considered gross income to the borrower and thus subject to individual income tax.

Reason for Change

At the time the loans are forgiven, the individuals who have met the requirements for debt forgiveness in the income-contingent and the income-based repayment programs would have been making payments for 25 years. In general, these individuals will have had low incomes relative to their debt burden for many years. For many of these individuals, paying the tax on the forgiven amounts will be difficult. Furthermore, the potential tax consequence may be making some student loan borrowers reluctant to accept forgiveness of the loan.

Proposal

The proposal would exclude from gross income amounts forgiven at the end of the repayment period for Federal student loans using the income-contingent repayment option or the incomebased repayment option.

The provision would be effective for loans forgiven after December 31, 2011.

TAX QUALIFIED DIVIDENDS AND NET LONG-TERM CAPITAL GAINS AT A 20-PERCENT RATE FOR UPPER-INCOME TAXPAYERS

Current Law

Under current law, the maximum rate of tax on the qualified dividends and net long-term capital gains of an individual is 15 percent. In addition, any qualified dividends and capital gains that would otherwise be taxed at a 10- or 15-percent ordinary income tax rate are taxed at a zero-percent rate. Gains from recapture of depreciation on certain real estate (section 1250) are taxed at ordinary rates up to 25 percent. Gains from the sale of collectibles are taxed at ordinary rates up to 28 percent. Special provisions also apply to gains from the sale of certain small business stock. The same rates apply for purposes of the alternative minimum tax.

Capital losses generally are deductible in full against capital gains. In addition, individual taxpayers may deduct up to $3,000 of capital losses from ordinary income each year. Any remaining unused capital losses may be carried forward indefinitely to a future year.

The zero- and 15-percent rates for qualified dividends and capital gains are scheduled to expire for taxable years beginning after December 31, 2012. In 2013, the maximum income tax rate on capital gains would increase to 20 percent (18 percent for assets purchased after December 31, 2000 and held longer than five years), while all dividends would be taxed at ordinary tax rates of up to 39.6 percent.

Reasons for Change

Taxing qualified dividends at the same low rate as capital gains for all taxpayers reduces the tax bias against equity investment and promotes a more efficient allocation of capital. Eliminating the special 18-percent rate on gains from assets held for more than five years further simplifies the tax code.

Proposal

The Administration's revenue baseline assumes that the current zero- and 15-percent tax rates for qualified dividends and net long-term net capital gains are permanently extended for middle-class taxpayers.

The proposal would apply a 20-percent tax rate on qualified dividends that would otherwise be taxed at a 36- or 39.6 percent ordinary income tax rate. This is the same rate as will apply to net long-term capital gains for upper-income taxpayers under current law after 2012. The reduced rates on gains from assets held over five years would be repealed. The special rates applying to recapture of depreciation on certain real estate (Section 1250 recapture) and collectibles would be retained.

This proposal would be effective for taxable years beginning after December 31, 2012.

TAX CUTS FOR BUSINESSES

ELIMINATE CAPITAL GAINS TAXATION ON INVESTMENTS IN SMALL BUSINESS STOCK

Current Law

Under the Small Business Jobs Act, taxpayers other than corporations may exclude 100 percent of the gain from the sale of qualified small business stock acquired after September 27, 2010 and before January 1, 2011, and held for at least five years, provided various requirements are met The Tax Relief, Unemployment Insurance Reauthorization and Job Creation Act of 2010 extended this 100 percent exclusion to eligible stock acquired before January 1, 2012.

The excluded gain is not a preference under the Alternative Minimum Tax (AMT) for stock acquired during this period. Prior law provided a 50 percent exclusion (60 percent for certain empowerment zone businesses) for qualified small business stock. The taxable portion of the gain is taxed at a maximum rate of 28 percent. The AMT treats 28 percent of the excluded gain on eligible stock acquired after December 31, 2000 and 42 percent of the excluded gain on stock acquired before January 1, 2001 as a tax preference. A 75 percent exclusion enacted under the American Recovery and Reinvestment Act (ARRA) applies to qualified stock acquired after February 17, 2009, and before September 28, 2010 with the excluded gains subject to the AMT.

The maximum amount of gain eligible for the exclusion by a taxpayer with respect to any corporation during any year is the greater of (1) ten times the taxpayer's basis in stock issued by the corporation and disposed of during the year, or (2) $10 million reduced by gain excluded in prior years on dispositions of the corporation's stock. To qualify as a small business, the corporation, when the stock is issued, may not have gross assets exceeding $50 million (including the proceeds of the newly issued stock) and must be a C corporation.

The corporation also must meet certain active trade or business requirements. For example, the corporation must be engaged in a trade or business other than: one involving the performance of services in the fields of health, law, engineering, architecture, accounting, actuarial science, performing arts, consulting, athletics, financial services, brokerage services or any other trade or business where the principal asset of the trade or business is the reputation or skill of one or more employees; a banking, insurance, financing, leasing, investing or similar business; a farming business; a business involving production or extraction of items subject to depletion; or a hotel, motel, restaurant or similar business. There are limits on the amount of real property that may be held by a qualified small business, and ownership of, dealing in, or renting real property is not treated as an active trade or business.

Reasons for Change

Making the exclusion permanent would encourage and reward new investment in qualified small business stock.

12

Proposal

The proposal would increase permanently to 100 percent the exclusion for qualified small business stock sold by an individual or other non-corporate taxpayer and would eliminate the AMT preference item for gain excluded under this provision. As under current law, the stock would have to be held for at least five years and other limitations on the section 1202 exclusion would continue to apply. The proposal would include additional documentation requirements to assure compliance with those limitations and taxpayers would be required to report qualified sales on their tax returns.

The proposal would be effective for qualified small business stock acquired after December 31, 2011.

ENHANCE AND MAKE PERMANENT THE RESEARCH AND EXPERIMENTATION (R&E) TAX CREDIT

Current Law

The R&E tax credit is 20 percent of qualified research expenses above a base amount. The base amount is the product of the taxpayer's "fixed base percentage" and the average of the taxpayer's gross receipts for the four preceding years. The taxpayer's fixed base percentage generally is the ratio of its research expenses to gross receipts for the 1984-88 period. The base amount cannot be less than 50 percent of the taxpayer's qualified research expenses for the taxable year. Taxpayers can elect the alternative simplified research credit (ASC), which is equal to 14 percent of qualified research expenses that exceed 50 percent of the average qualified research expenses for the three preceding taxable years. Under the ASC, the rate is reduced to 6 percent if a taxpayer has no qualified research expenses in any one of the three preceding taxable years. An election to use the ASC applies to all succeeding taxable years unless revoked with the consent of the Secretary.

The R&E tax credit also provides a credit for 20 percent of: (1) basic research payments above a base amount; and (2) all eligible payments to an energy research consortium for energy research.

The R&E tax credit is scheduled to expire on December 31, 2011.

Reasons for Change

The R&E tax credit encourages technological developments that are an important component of economic growth. However, uncertainty about the future availability of the R&E tax credit diminishes the incentive effect of the credit because it is difficult for taxpayers to factor the credit into decisions to invest in research projects that will not be initiated and completed prior to the credit's expiration. To improve the credit's effectiveness, the R&E tax credit should be made permanent.

Currently, a taxpayer must choose between using an outdated formula for calculating the R&E credit that provides a 20-percent credit rate for research spending over a certain base amount related to the business's historical research intensity and the much simpler ASC that provides a 14-percent credit in excess of a base amount based on its recent research spending. Increasing the rate of the ASC to 17 percent would provide an improved incentive to increase research and would make the ASC a more attractive alternative. Because the ASC base is updated annually, the ASC more accurately reflects the business's recent research experience and simplifies the R&E credit's computation.

Proposal

The proposal would make the R&E credit permanent and increase the rate of the alternative simplified research credit from 14 percent to 17 percent, effective after December 31, 2011.

PROVIDE ADDITIONAL TAX CREDITS FOR INVESTMENT IN QUALIFIED PROPERTY USED IN A QUALIFYING ADVANCED ENERGY MANUFACTURING PROJECT ("48C")

Current Law

A 30-percent tax credit is provided for investments in eligible property used in a qualifying advanced energy project. A qualifying advanced energy project is a project that re-equips, expands, or establishes a manufacturing facility for the production of: (1) property designed to produce energy from renewable resources; (2) fuel cells, microturbines, or an energy storage system for use with electric or hybrid-electric vehicles; (3) electric grids to support the transmission, including storage, of intermittent sources of renewable energy; (4) property designed to capture and sequester carbon dioxide emissions; (5) property designed to refine or blend renewable fuels or to produce energy conservation technologies; (6) electric drive motor vehicles that qualify for tax credits or components designed for use with such vehicles; and (7) other advanced energy property designed to reduce greenhouse gas emissions.

Eligible property is property: (1) that is necessary for the production of the property listed above; (2) that is tangible personal property or other tangible property (not including a building and its structural components) that is used as an integral part of a qualifying facility; and (3) with respect to which depreciation (or amortization in lieu of depreciation) is allowable.

Under the American Recovery and Reinvestment Act of 2009 (ARRA), total credits were limited to $2.3 billion, and the Treasury Department, in consultation with the Department of Energy, was required to establish a program to consider and award certifications for qualified investments eligible for credits within 180 days of the date of enactment of ARRA. Credits may be allocated only to projects where there is a reasonable expectation of commercial viability. In addition, consideration must be given to which projects: (1) will provide the greatest domestic job creation; (2) will have the greatest net impact in avoiding or reducing air pollutants or greenhouse gas emissions; (3) have the greatest potential for technological innovation and commercial deployment; (4) have the lowest levelized cost of generated or stored energy, or of measured reduction in energy consumption or greenhouse gas emission; and (5) have the shortest completion time. Guidance under current law requires taxpayers to apply for the credit with respect to their entire qualified investment in a project.

Applications for certification under the program may be made only during the two-year period beginning on the date the program is established. An applicant that is allocated credits must provide evidence that the requirements of the certification have been met within one year of the date of acceptance of the application and must place the property in service within three years from the date of the issuance of the certification.

Reasons for Change

The $2.3 billion cap on the credit has resulted in the funding of less than one-third of the technically acceptable applications that have been received. Rather than turning down worthy projects that could be deployed quickly to create jobs and support economic activity, the program – which has proven successful in leveraging private investment in building and equipping factories that manufacture clean energy products in America – should be expanded. An additional $5 billion in credits would support at least $15 billion in total capital investment, creating tens of thousands of new construction and manufacturing jobs. Because there is already an existing pipeline of worthy projects and substantial interest in this area, the additional credit can be deployed quickly to create jobs and support economic activity.

Proposal

The proposal would authorize an additional $5 billion of credits for investments in eligible property used in a qualifying advanced energy manufacturing project. Taxpayers would be able to apply for a credit with respect to only part of their qualified investment. If a taxpayer applies for a credit with respect to only part of the qualified investment in the project, the taxpayer's increased cost sharing and the project's reduced revenue cost to the government would be taken into account in determining whether to allocate credits to the project.

Applications for the additional credits would be made during the two-year period beginning on the date on which the additional authorization is enacted. As under current law, applicants that are allocated the additional credits must provide evidence that the requirements of the certification have been met within one year of the date of acceptance of the application and must place the property in service within three years from the date of the issuance of the certification.

The change would be effective on the date of enactment.

PROVIDE TAX CREDIT FOR ENERGY-EFFICIENT COMMERCIAL BUILDING PROPERTY EXPENDITURES IN PLACE OF EXISTING TAX DEDUCTION

Current Law

Under section 179D of the Internal Revenue Code, taxpayers are allowed to deduct expenditures for energy efficient commercial building property. Energy efficient commercial building property is defined as property (1) which is installed on or in any building that is located in the United States and is within the scope of Standard 90.1-2001, (2) which is installed as part of (i) the interior lighting systems, (ii) the heating, cooling, ventilation, and hot water systems, or (iii) the building envelope, (3) which is certified as being installed as part of a plan designed to reduce the total annual energy and power costs with respect to the interior lighting, heating, cooling, ventilation, and hot water systems of the building by 50 percent or more in comparison to a reference building which meets the minimum requirements of Standard 90.1-2001, and (4) with respect to which depreciation (or amortization in lieu of depreciation) is allowable. Standard 90.1-2001, as referred to here, is Standard 90.1-2001 of the American Society of Heating, Refrigerating, and Air Conditioning Engineers and the Illuminating Engineering Society of North America (ASHRAE/IESNA) as in effect on April 2, 2003 – a nationally accepted building energy code that has been adopted by local and state jurisdictions throughout the United States. The deduction with respect to a building is limited to $1.80 per square foot.

In the case of a building that does not achieve a 50-percent energy savings, a partial deduction is allowed with respect to each separate building system (interior lighting; heating cooling, ventilation, and hot water; and building envelope) that meets the system-specific energy-savings target prescribed by the Secretary of the Treasury. The applicable system-specific savings targets are those that would result in a total annual energy savings with respect to the whole building of 50 percent, if each of the separate systems met the system-specific target. The maximum allowable deduction for each of the separate systems is $0.60 per square foot.

The deduction is allowed in the year in which the property is placed in service. If the energy efficient commercial building property expenditures are made by a public entity, the deduction may be allocated under regulations to the person primarily responsible for designing the property. The deduction applies to property placed in service on or before December 31, 2013.

Reasons for Change

The President has called for a new Better Buildings Initiative that would over 10 years reduce energy usage in commercial buildings by 20 percent. This initiative would catalyze private sector investment in upgrading the efficiency of commercial buildings. Changing the current tax deduction for energy efficient commercial building property to a tax credit and allowing a partial credit for achieving less stringent efficiency standards would encourage private sector investments in energy efficiency improvements. In addition, allowing a credit based on prescriptive efficiency standards would reduce the complexity of the current standards, which require whole-building auditing, modeling and simulation.

Proposal

The proposal would replace the existing deduction for energy efficient commercial building property with a tax credit equal to the cost of property that is certified as being installed as part of a plan designed to reduce the total annual energy and power costs with respect to the interior lighting, heating, cooling, ventilation, and hot water systems of the building by 20 percent or more in comparison to a reference building which meets the minimum requirements of ASHR2AE/IESNA Standard 90.1-2004, as in effect on the date of enactment.

The credit with respect to a building would be limited to $0.60 per square foot in the case of energy efficient commercial building property designed to reduce the total annual energy and power costs by at least 20 percent but less than 30 percent, to $0.90 per square foot for qualifying property designed to reduce the total annual energy and power costs by at least 30 percent but less than 50 percent, and to $1.80 per square foot for qualifying property designed to reduce the total annual energy and power costs by 50 percent or more.

In addition, the proposal would treat property as meeting the 20-, 30-, and 50-percent energy savings requirement if specified prescriptive standards are satisfied. Prescriptive standards would be based on building types (as specified by Standard 90.1-2004) and climate zones (as specified by Standard 90.1-2004).

Special rules would be provided that would allow the credit to benefit a REIT or its shareholders.

The tax credit would be available for property placed in service during calendar year 2012.

INCENTIVES TO PROMOTE REGIONAL GROWTH

EXTEND AND MODIFY THE NEW MARKETS TAX CREDIT (NMTC)

Current Law

The NMTC is a 39-percent credit for qualified equity investments (QEIs) made to acquire stock in a corporation, or a capital interest in a partnership, that is a qualified community development entity (CDE) that is held for a period of seven years. The allowable credit amount for any given year is the applicable percentage (5 percent for the year the equity interest is purchased from the CDE and for each of the two subsequent years, and 6 percent for each of the following four years) of the amount paid to the CDE for the investment at its original issue. The NMTC is available for a taxable year to the taxpayer who holds the qualified equity investment on the date of the initial investment or on the respective anniversary date that occurs during the taxable year. The credit is recaptured if at any time during the seven-year period that begins on the date of the original issue of the investment the entity ceases to be a qualified CDE, the proceeds of the investment cease to be used as required, or the equity investment is redeemed.

Under current law, the NMTC can be used to offset federal income tax liability but cannot be used to offset alternative minimum tax (AMT) liability.

The NMTC will expire on December 31, 2011.

Reasons for Change

An extension of the NMTC would allow CDEs to continue to generate investments in low-income communities.

Proposal

The proposal would extend the new markets tax credit for one year (2012), with an allocation amount of $5.0 billion. The Administration estimates that within this $5 billion, at least $250 million will support financing healthy food options in distressed communities as part of the Healthy Food Financing Initiative. The proposal also would permit NMTC amounts resulting from QEIs made after December 31, 2010, to offset AMT liability.

The proposal would be effective upon enactment.

REFORM AND EXTEND BUILD AMERICA BONDS

Current Law

Build America Bonds are a new borrowing tool for State and local governments that were enacted as part of the American Recovery and Reinvestment Act of 2009 (ARRA). These bonds are conventional taxable bonds issued by State and local governments. The Treasury Department makes direct payments to State and local governmental issuers (called "refundable tax credits") to subsidize a portion of their borrowing costs in an amount equal to 35 percent of the coupon interest on the bonds. Issuance of Build America Bonds is limited to original financing for public capital projects for which issuers otherwise could use tax-exempt "governmental bonds" (as contrasted with "private activity bonds" which benefit private entities.) ARRA authorized the issuance of Build America Bonds in 2009 and 2010 without volume limitation and authority to issue these bonds expired at the end of 2010. Build America Bonds are an optional alternative to traditional tax-exempt bonds.

Tax-exempt bonds have broader program parameters than Build America Bonds, and may be used in the following ways: (1) original financing for public capital projects, as with Build America Bonds; (2) "current refundings" to refinance prior governmental bonds for interest cost savings where the prior bonds are repaid promptly within ninety days of issuance of the refunding bonds (as well as one "advance refunding," in which two sets of bonds for the same governmental purpose may remain outstanding concurrently for a period of time longer than ninety days); (3) short-term "working capital" financings for governmental operating expenses for seasonal cash flow deficits (as well as certain longer-term deficit financings which have strict arbitrage restrictions); (4) financing for Code 501(c)(3) nonprofit entities, such as nonprofit hospitals and universities; and (5) qualified private activity bond financing for specified private projects and programs (including, for example, mass commuting facilities, solid waste disposal facilities, low-income residential rental housing projects, and single-family housing for low and moderate income homebuyers, among others), which are subject to annual state bond volume caps with certain exceptions.

Reasons for Change

The Build America Bond program has been successful and has expanded the market for State and local governmental debt. From April 2009 through December 2010, more than $181 billion in Build America Bonds were issued in over 2,275 transactions in all 50 States, the District of Columbia, and two territories. During 2009-2010, Build America Bonds gained a market share of over 25 percent of the total dollar supply of State and local governmental debt. This program taps into a broader market for investors without regard to tax liability (e.g., pension funds may be investors in Build America Bonds, though they typically do not invest in tax-exempt bonds). By comparison, traditional tax-exempt bonds have a narrower class of investors with tax preferences, which generally consist of retail investors (individuals and mutual funds hold over 70 percent of tax-exempt bonds). This program delivers an efficient Federal subsidy directly to State and local governments (rather than through third-party investors). By comparison, tax-exempt bonds can be viewed as inefficient in that the Federal revenue cost of the tax exemption is often greater than the benefits to State and local governments achieved through lower borrowing costs. This program also has a potentially more streamlined tax compliance framework focusing directly on governmental issuers who benefit from the subsidy, as compared with tax-exempt bonds and tax credit bonds which involve investors as tax intermediaries. This program also has relieved supply pressures in the tax-exempt bond market and has helped to reduce interest rates in that market. Making the Build America Bond program permanent could promote market certainty and greater liquidity.

The 35-percent Federal subsidy rate for the original Build America Bond program represented a deeper Federal borrowing subsidy for temporary stimulus purposes under ARRA than the existing permanent Federal subsidy inherent in tax-exempt bonds. In structuring a permanent Build America Bond program in light of Federal revenue constraints, it is appropriate to develop a revenue neutral Federal subsidy rate relative to the Federal tax expenditure on tax-exempt bonds.

For such a revenue neutral Federal subsidy rate, it also is appropriate to expand the eligible uses for Build America Bonds to include other program purposes for which tax-exempt bonds may be used.

Proposal

Permanent Program for Build America Bonds. This proposal would make the Build America Bonds program permanent at a Federal subsidy level equal to 28 percent of the coupon interest on the bonds. The proposed Federal subsidy level is intended to be approximately revenue neutral relative to the estimated future Federal tax expenditure for tax-exempt bonds. A permanent Build America Bonds program should facilitate greater efficiency, a broader investor base, and lower costs for State and local governmental debt.

Expanded Uses. This proposal would also expand the eligible uses for Build America Bonds to include the following: (1) original financing for governmental capital projects, as under the initial authorization of Build America Bonds; (2) current refundings of prior public capital project financings for interest cost savings where the prior bonds are repaid promptly within ninety days of issuance of the current refunding bonds; (3) short-term governmental working capital financings for governmental operating expenses (such as tax and revenue anticipation borrowings for seasonal cash flow deficits), subject to a thirteen-month maturity limitation; and (4) financing for Section 501(c)(3) nonprofit entities, such as nonprofit hospitals and universities.

This proposal would be effective for bonds issued after the date of enactment.

Low-Income Housing Tax Credit (LIHTC) Provisions

ENCOURAGE MIXED-INCOME OCCUPANCY BY ALLOWING LIHTC-SUPPORTED PROJECTS TO ELECT AN AVERAGE-INCOME CRITERION

Current law

In order for a building to qualify for the LIHTC, a minimum portion of the units in the building must be rent restricted and occupied by low-income tenants. Under section 42(g)(1), the taxpayer makes an irrevocable election between two criteria. Either—

- At least 20 percent of the units must be rent restricted and occupied by tenants with income at or below 50 percent of area median income (AMI); or

- At least 40 percent of the units must be rent restricted and occupied by tenants with incomes at or below 60 percent of AMI.

In all cases, qualifying income standards are adjusted for family size. The amount of the credit reflects the fraction of the building's eligible basis that is attributable to the low-income units.

Reasons for change

In practice, these criteria often produce buildings that serve a very narrow income band of tenants—those just below the top of the eligible income range. For example, if the rent-restricted units in the building must be occupied by tenants at or below 60 percent of AMI, these units may end up being occupied by tenants with incomes that fall between 54 percent and 60 percent of AMI. As a result, the income criteria do not include incentives to create mixed-income housing, and LIHTC-supported buildings often do not serve those most in need. In addition, the inflexibility of the income criteria makes it difficult for LIHTC to support acquisition of partially or fully occupied properties for preservation or repurposing.

Proposal

The proposal would add a third criterion to the two described above. When a taxpayer elects this criterion, at least 40 percent of the units would have to be occupied by tenants with incomes that *average* no more than 60 percent of AMI. No rent-restricted unit, however, could be occupied by a tenant with income over 80 percent of AMI; and, for purposes of computing the average, any unit with an income limit that is less than 20 percent of AMI would be treated as having a 20-percent limit.

For example, suppose that a building had 10 rent-restricted units with income limits of 20 percent of AMI, 10 with limits of 40 percent of AMI, 20 with limits of 60 percent of AMI, and 30 with limits of 80 percent of AMI. This would satisfy the new criterion because none of the limits exceeds 80 percent of AMI and the average does not exceed 60 percent of AMI. ($10 \times 20 + 10 \times 40 + 20 \times 60 + 30 \times 80 = 4200$, and $4200/70 = 60$.)

The proposal would be effective for elections under section 42(g)(1) that are made after the date of enactment.

PROVIDE 30-PERCENT BASIS "BOOST" TO PROPERTIES THAT RECEIVE TAX-EXEMPT BOND FINANCING

Current law

Subject to certain adjustments and special rules, eligible basis for computing LIHTC is generally a building's adjusted basis. In some situations, however, there is an increase (a "basis boost") over the amount that would otherwise be eligible basis. For example, if the State housing credit agency designates a building as needing an enhanced credit in order to be financially feasible as part of a qualified low-income housing project, then the eligible basis for the building may be up to 130 percent of what it would be in the absence of any such boost. This basis boost is not available, however, for a building if any portion of the eligible basis of the building is financed by tax-exempt bonds subject to the private-activity-bond volume cap (volume cap).

Reasons for Change

Preservation of existing affordable housing is acutely needed. Many tens of thousands of federally assisted housing units are being lost, in large part because of inability to fund necessary capital improvements. LIHTC-supported preservation offers the hope not only of protecting the existing Federal investment in affordable housing by leveraging private capital but also of gaining the benefits of private-market discipline for Federally assisted properties. Moreover, preservation is a cost-effective alternative to new construction. The per-unit cost of preservation is about one quarter that of new construction, and it greatly reduces the financial and human costs of relocating tenants.

As currently structured, however, the LIHTC does not attract sufficient equity capital to address preservation needs. Historically, the 70-percent-present-value credit (colloquially called the "9-percent credit") has been oversubscribed, with proposals for new construction tending to beat out those for preservation. The 30-percent-present-value credit (colloquially called the "4-percent credit") often fails to provide sufficient incentive to make preservation projects economically attractive.

Proposal

The proposal would allow State housing finance agencies to designate certain projects to receive, for purposes of computing LIHTC, a 30 percent boost in eligible basis. To receive this treatment, a project would have to satisfy the following requirements:

- The project involves the preservation, recapitalization, and rehabilitation of existing housing;

- The housing demonstrates a serious backlog of capital needs or deferred maintenance;

- At least half of the aggregate basis of the building and of the land on which the building is located is financed by tax-exempt bonds that are subject to the volume cap;

- The project involves housing that was previously financed with Federal funds (including having benefited from LIHTC); and

23

- Because of that funding, the housing was subject to a long-term use agreement limiting occupancy to low-income households.

The volume of designations that a State housing finance agency can make would be limited by an amount that is computed using the State's volume cap. The limitation applicable to a project would depend on the calendar year of issue of the tax-exempt bonds that help finance the project and not on which year's volume cap was taken into account in issuing the bonds. Under the limitation, the aggregate issue price of the bonds that are issued in a calendar year and that finance projects whose bases are designated for a boost under this provision would not be allowed to exceed an amount equal to 0.4 percent of the State's volume cap for that calendar year. Thus, for example, if an otherwise-qualifying project is financed with tax-exempt bonds that are issued in 2012 using volume cap that the state carried over from 2010, the basis boost for that project would be subject to a limitation that is based on an amount equal to 0.4 percent of the State's volume cap for 2012.

The proposal would be effective for projects that are financed by tax-exempt bonds issued after the date of enactment.

DESIGNATE GROWTH ZONES

Current Law

The Internal Revenue Code contains various incentives targeted to encourage the development of particular geographic regions, including empowerment zones and the Gulf Opportunity (GO) Zone. In addition, qualifying investment placed in service in 2011 and 2012 is eligible for additional first-year depreciation of the adjusted basis of the property.

Empowerment Zones

There are currently 40 empowerment zones—30 in urban areas and 10 in rural areas—that have been designated through a competitive application process in three separate rounds in 1994, 1998, and 2002.[1] State and local governments nominated distressed geographic areas, which were selected on the strength of their strategic plans for economic and social revitalization. The urban areas were designated by the Secretary of Housing and Urban Development. The rural areas were designated by the Secretary of Agriculture. Empowerment zone designation remains in effect through December 31, 2011.

Incentives for businesses in empowerment zones include (1) a 20-percent wage credit for qualifying wages, (2) additional expensing for qualified zone property, (3) tax-exempt financing for certain qualifying zone facilities, (4) deferral of capital gains on sales and reinvestment in empowerment zone assets, and (5) exclusion of 60 percent (rather than 50 percent) of the gain on the sale of qualified small business stock held more than 5 years.[2]

The wage credit provides a 20 percent subsidy on the first $15,000 of annual wages paid to residents of empowerment zones by businesses located in these communities, if substantially all of the employee's services are performed within the zone. The credit is not available for wages taken into account in determining the work opportunity tax credit.

To be eligible for the capital incentives, businesses must generally satisfy the requirements of an enterprise zone business. Among other conditions, these requirements stipulate that at least 50 percent of the total gross income of such business is derived from the active conduct of a business within an empowerment zone, a substantial portion of the use of tangible property of such business is within an empowerment zone, and at least 35 percent of its employees are residents of an empowerment zone.

Enterprise zone businesses are allowed to expense the cost of certain qualified zone property (which, among other requirements, must be used in the active conduct of a qualified business in an empowerment zone) up to an additional $35,000 above the amounts generally available under

---

[1] In addition, the District of Columbia Enterprise Zone (DC Zone) was established in 1998 and receives similar tax benefits to empowerment zones. The primary differences are that the eligibility rules are more generous for the DC Zone, the capital gains preferences are in the form of a full exclusion from income on the gain from qualified DC Zone assets held more than 5 years, and a homebuyer credit is provided to first-time homebuyers within DC. DC Zone status remains in effect through December 31, 2011.

[2] For qualified small business stock acquired after September 27, 2010 and before January 1, 2012, the exclusion percentage increases to 100 percent. This provision (100 percent exclusion) applies to all qualified small business stock, not just that issued by enterprise zone businesses.

section 179.[3] In addition, only 50 percent of the cost of such qualified zone property counts toward the limitation under which section 179 deductions are reduced to the extent the cost of section 179 property exceeds a specified amount.

Qualified enterprise zone businesses are eligible to apply for tax-exempt financing (empowerment zone facility bonds) for qualified zone property. These empowerment zone facility bonds do not count against state private activity bond limits; instead a limit is placed upon each zone, depending on population and whether the zone is in an urban or rural area.

In addition, residents of empowerment zones aged 18-39 years old qualify as a targeted group for the work opportunity tax credit (WOTC). Employers who hire an individual in a targeted group receive a 40 percent credit that applies to the first $6,000 of qualified first-year wages. Empowerment zone residents aged 16-17 can also qualify as a targeted group for WOTC, but the qualifying wage limit is reduced to $3,000 and the period of employment must be between May 1 and September 15.

GO Zone

The GO Zone is the portion of the Hurricane Katrina disaster area determined by the President to warrant individual or individual and public assistance from the Federal Government under the Robert T. Stafford Disaster Relief and Emergency Assistance Act by reason of Hurricane Katrina in 2005. Numerous tax incentives were provided to encourage the redevelopment of the areas within the GO zone, most of which have expired. Provisions still in effect through 2011 include an increase in available tax-exempt bond financing, an increase in the allocation of low-income housing tax credits, an increase in the rehabilitation credit rate for structures located in the GO Zone, and an additional first-year depreciation deduction for qualified property described below.

An additional first-year depreciation deduction is allowed for specified GO Zone extension property placed in service prior to January 1, 2012. The deduction equals 50 percent of the cost of qualified property. Specified GO Zone extension property is defined as property substantially all the use of which is in one or more specified portions of the GO Zone. Qualifying property must either be (1) nonresidential real property or residential rental property, or (2) in the case of a taxpayer who places in service a building described in (1), tangible personal property contained in the building as described in section 168(k)(2)(A)(i), if substantially all the use of such property is in such building and such property is placed in service within 90 days of the date the building is placed in service. The specified portions of the GO Zone are defined as those portions of the GO Zone which is identified by the Secretary of the Treasury as being in a county or parish in which hurricanes occurring in 2005 damaged more than 60 percent of the occupied housing units in such county or parish.

---

[3] Section 179 provides that, in place of depreciation, certain taxpayers, typically small businesses, may elect to deduct up to $500,000 of the cost of section 179 property placed in service in 2011. In general, section 179 property is defined as including depreciable tangible personal property, certain depreciable real property (not including a building, or its structural components), and (through 2013) certain computer software. In 2011, section 179 property also includes up to $250,000 of certain qualified real property (which includes leasehold improvement property, restaurant property, and retail improvement property). Section 179 property must be purchased for use in the active conduct of a trade or business.

Bonus Depreciation

An additional first-year depreciation deduction is allowed for qualified property placed in service during 2011 and 2012. The deduction equals 100 percent of the cost of qualified property placed in service in 2011 and 50 percent of the cost of qualified property placed in service in 2012, and is allowed for both regular tax and alternative minimum tax purposes. The property's depreciable basis is adjusted to reflect this additional deduction. However, the taxpayer may elect out of additional first-year depreciation for any class of property for any taxable year.

Qualified property for this purpose includes tangible property with a recovery period of 20 years or less, water utility property, certain computer software, and qualified leasehold improvement property. Qualified property must be new property, and excludes property that is required to be depreciated under the alternative depreciation system (ADS). To qualify for the 50 percent additional first-year depreciation deduction, property must be (1) acquired after December 31, 2007 and before January 1, 2013 (but only if no written binding contract for the acquisition was in effect before January 1, 2008), or (2) acquired pursuant to a written binding contract entered into after December 31, 2007, and before January 1, 2013. In general, the property must be placed in service by January 1, 2013. If property is self-constructed, the taxpayer must begin manufacture or construction of the property after December 31, 2007 and before January 1, 2013. To qualify for the 100 percent additional first-year deduction, the property must be acquired after September 8, 2010 and before January 1, 2012, and placed in service before January 1, 2012. An extension by one year of the placed-in-service date is allowed for certain property with a recovery period of ten years or longer and certain transportation property, if the property has an estimated production period exceeding one year and a cost exceeding $1 million. Certain aircraft not used in providing transportation services are also granted a one-year extension of the placed-in-service deadline. In these cases, the additional allowance applies only to adjusted basis attributable to manufacture or construction occurring before January 1, 2013. Special rules apply to syndications, sale-leasebacks, and transfers to related parties of qualified property.

Corporations otherwise eligible for additional first-year depreciation may elect to claim additional research or minimum tax credits in lieu of claiming additional depreciation for "eligible qualified property." Such property only includes otherwise qualified property that was acquired after March 31, 2008, but only taking into account adjusted basis attributable to the manufacture or construction of the property either (1) after March 31, 2008 and before January 1, 2010, or (2) after December 31, 2010, and before January 1, 2013. Only additional minimum tax credits may be taken with respect to property qualifying under (2). Depreciation for eligible qualified property must be computed using the straight-line method.

Reasons for Change

Growth zones would promote job creation and investment in economically distressed areas that have demonstrated potential for future growth and diversification into new industries. While current law provides regionally targeted benefits to numerous areas, these incentives are due to expire soon and some of these designations have been in effect over 16 years. The Administration desires to target resources to areas where they would provide the most benefit on a going-forward basis. In particular, the national competition for growth zone status would drivers of regional economic growth. The targeted tax incentives provided to the zone would encourage private sector investment and other forms of increased economic activity in these areas. The current tax incentives are perceived as complex and difficult for businesses to navigate, potentially reducing the take-up rate for these incentives.

Proposal

The Administration proposes to designate 20 growth zones (14 in urban areas and 6 in rural areas). The zone designation and corresponding tax incentives would be in effect from January 1, 2012 through December 31, 2016. The Secretary of Commerce would select the zones in consultation with the Secretary of Housing and Urban Development and the Secretary of Agriculture.

The zones would be chosen through a competitive application process. A State, county, city, or other general purpose political subdivision of a State or possession (a "local government"), or an Indian tribal government would be eligible to nominate an area for growth zone status. Areas could be nominated by more than one local government, if the nominated area is within the jurisdiction of more than one local government or State. In addition, local governments within a region could join together to jointly nominate multiple areas for growth zone status, so long as each designated zone independently satisfies the eligibility criteria. To be eligible to be nominated, an area must satisfy the following criteria:

1. A nominated area would have to have a continuous boundary (that is, an area must be a single area; it cannot be comprised of two or more separate areas) and could not exceed 20 square miles if an urban area or 1,000 square miles if a rural area.

2. A nominated urban area would have to include a portion of at least one local government jurisdiction with a population of at least 50,000. The population of a nominated urban area could not exceed the lesser of: (1) 200,000; or (2) the greater of 50,000 or ten percent of the population of the most populous city in the nominated area. A nominated rural area could not have a population that exceeded 30,000.

Nominated areas would be designated as growth zones based on the strength of the applicant's "competitiveness plan" and its need to attract investment and jobs. Communities would be encouraged to develop a strategic plan to build on their economic strengths and outline targeted investments to develop their competitive advantages. Collaboration across a wide range of stakeholders would be useful in developing a coherent and comprehensive strategic plan. A successful plan would clearly outline how the economic strategy would connect the zone to drivers of regional economic growth.

In evaluating applications, the Secretary of Commerce could consider other factors, including: unemployment rates, poverty rates, household income, homeownership, labor force participation and educational attainment. In addition, the Secretary may set minimal standards for the levels of unemployment and poverty that must be satisfied by the nominated area.

"Rural area" would be defined as any area that is (1) outside of a metropolitan statistical area (within the meaning of section 143(k)(2)(B)) or (2) determined by the Secretary of Commerce, after consultation with the Secretary of Agriculture, to be a rural area. "Urban area" would be defined as any area that is not a rural area.

Two tax incentives would be applicable to growth zones. First, an employment credit would be provided to businesses that employ zone residents. The credit would apply to the first $15,000 of qualifying zone employee wages. The credit rate would be 20 percent for zone residents who are employed within the zone and 10 percent for zone residents employed outside of the zone. The definition of a qualified zone employee would follow rules found in section 1396(d). For the purposes of the 10 percent credit, the requirement that substantially all of the services performed by the employee for the employer are within the zone would not apply. The definition of qualified zone wages would follow the definitions provided in section 1396(c) and 1397(a).

Second, qualified property placed in service within the zone would be eligible for additional first-year depreciation of 100 percent of the adjusted basis of the property. Qualified property for this purpose includes tangible property with a recovery period of 20 years or less, water utility property, certain computer software, and qualified leasehold improvement property. Qualified property must be new property. Qualified property excludes property that is required to be depreciated under the ADS. The taxpayer must purchase (or begin the manufacture or construction of) the property after the date of zone designation and before January 1, 2017 (but only if no written binding contract for the acquisition was in effect before zone designation). The property must be placed in service within the zone before January 1, 2017.

The Secretary of the Treasury would be given authority to collect data from taxpayers on the use of such tax incentives by zone. The Secretary of Commerce may require the nominating local government to provide other data on the economic conditions in the zones both before and after designation. These data would be used to evaluate the effectiveness of the growth zones program.

RESTRUCTURE ASSISTANCE TO NEW YORK CITY: PROVIDE TAX INCENTIVES FOR TRANSPORTATION INFRASTRUCTURE

Current Law

The Job Creation and Worker Assistance Act of 2002 (the Act) provided tax incentives for the area of New York City damaged or affected by the terrorist attacks on September 11, 2001. The Act created the "New York Liberty Zone," defined as the area located on or south of Canal Street, East Broadway (east of its intersection with Canal Street), or Grand Street (east of its intersection with East Broadway) in the Borough of Manhattan in the City of New York, New York. New York Liberty Zone tax incentives included: (1) an expansion of the work opportunity tax credit (WOTC) for New York Liberty Zone business employees; (2) a special depreciation allowance for qualified New York Liberty Zone property; (3) a five-year recovery period for depreciation of qualified New York Liberty Zone leasehold improvement property; (4) $8 billion of tax-exempt private activity bond financing for certain nonresidential real property, residential rental property and public utility property; (5) $9 billion of additional tax-exempt, advance refunding bonds; (6) increased section 179 expensing; and (7) an extension of the replacement period for nonrecognition of gain for certain involuntary conversions.[4]

The expanded WOTC credit provided a 40-percent subsidy on the first $6,000 of annual wages paid to New York Liberty Zone business employees for work performed during 2002 or 2003.

The special depreciation allowance for qualified New York Liberty Zone property equals 30 percent of the adjusted basis of the property for the taxable year in which the property was placed in service. Qualified nonresidential real property and residential rental property must have been purchased by the taxpayer after September 10, 2001, and placed in service before January 1, 2010. Such property is qualified property only to the extent it rehabilitates real property damaged, or replaces real property destroyed or condemned, as a result of the September 11, 2001, terrorist attacks.[5]

The five-year recovery period for qualified leasehold improvement property applied, in general, to buildings located in the New York Liberty Zone if the improvement was placed in service after September 10, 2001, and before January 1, 2007, and no written binding contract for the improvement was in effect before September 11, 2001.

The $8 billion of tax-exempt private activity bond financing is authorized to be issued by the State of New York or any political subdivision thereof after March 9, 2002, and before January 1, 2012.

The $9 billion of additional tax-exempt, advance refunding bonds was available after March 9, 2002, and before January 1, 2006, with respect to certain State or local bonds outstanding on September 11, 2001.

---

[4] The Working Families Tax Relief Act of 2004 amended certain of the New York Liberty Zone provisions relating to tax-exempt bonds.

[5] Other qualified property must have been placed in service prior to January 1, 2007.

Businesses were allowed to expense the cost of certain qualified New York Liberty Zone property placed in service prior to 2007, up to an additional $35,000 above the amounts generally available under section 179. In addition, only 50 percent of the cost of such qualified New York Liberty Zone property counted toward the limitation under which section 179 deductions are reduced to the extent the cost of section 179 property exceeds a specified amount.

A taxpayer may elect not to recognize gain with respect to property that is involuntarily converted if the taxpayer acquires within an applicable period (the replacement period) property similar or related in service or use. In general, the replacement period begins with the date of the disposition of the converted property and ends two years (three years if the converted property is real property held for the productive use in a trade or business or for investment) after the close of the first taxable year in which any part of the gain upon conversion is realized. The Act extended the replacement period to five years for property in the New York Liberty Zone that was involuntarily converted as a result of the terrorist attacks on September 11, 2001, if substantially all of the use of the replacement property is in New York City.

Reasons for Change

Some of the tax benefits that were provided to New York following the attacks of September 11, 2001, likely will not be usable in the form in which they were originally provided. State and local officials in New York have concluded that improvements to transportation infrastructure and connectivity in the Liberty Zone would have a greater impact on recovery and continued development than would continuing some of the original tax incentives.

Proposal

The proposal would provide tax credits to New York State and New York City for expenditures relating to the construction or improvement of transportation infrastructure in or connecting to the New York Liberty Zone. New York State and New York City each would be eligible for a tax credit for expenditures relating to the construction or improvement of transportation infrastructure in or connecting to the New York Liberty Zone. The tax credit would be allowed in each year from 2012 to 2021, inclusive, subject to an annual limit of $200 million (for a total of $2 billion in tax credits), and would be divided evenly between the State and the City. Any unused credits below the annual limit would be added to the $200 million annual limit for the following year, including years after 2021. Similarly, expenditures that exceed the annual limit would be carried forward and subtracted from the annual limit in the following year. The credit would be allowed against any payments (other than payments of excise taxes and social security and Medicare payroll taxes) made by the City and State under any provision of the Code, including income tax withholding. The Treasury Department would prescribe such rules as are necessary to ensure that the expenditures are made for the intended purposes. The amount of the credit received would be considered State and local funds for the purpose of any Federal program.

The proposal would be effective after December 31, 2011.

CONTINUE CERTAIN EXPIRING PROVISIONS THROUGH CALENDAR YEAR 2012

A number of temporary tax provisions that have been routinely extended have expired or are scheduled to expire on or before December 31, 2011. The Administration proposes to extend a number of these provisions through December 31, 2012. For example, the optional deduction for State and local general sales taxes; the deduction for qualified out-of-pocket classroom expenses; the deduction for qualified tuition and related expenses; the Subpart F "active financing" and "look-through" exceptions; the modified recovery period for qualified leasehold, restaurant, and retail improvements; and several trade agreements would be extended through December 31, 2012. Temporary incentives provided for the production of fossil fuels would be allowed to expire as scheduled under current law.

See Table 4 for a list of the provisions that the Administration proposes to extend.

OTHER REVENUE CHANGES AND LOOPHOLE CLOSERS

Reform Treatment of Financial Institutions and Products

IMPOSE A FINANCIAL CRISIS RESPONSIBILITY FEE

Current Law

There is no sector-specific Federal tax applied to financial firms (although these firms are subject to the general corporate income tax and potentially a wide range of excise taxes). Financial sector firms are subject to a range of fees, depending on the lines of business in which they participate. For example, banks are assessed fees by the Federal Deposit Insurance Corporation to cover the costs of insuring deposits made at these institutions.

Reasons for Change

Excessive risk undertaken by major financial firms was a significant cause of the recent financial crisis. Extraordinary steps were taken by the Federal government to inject funds into the financial system, guarantee certain types of securities, and purchase securities from weakened firms. The law which enabled some of these actions and which created the Troubled Asset Relief Program (TARP) requires the President to propose an assessment on the financial sector to pay back the costs of these extraordinary actions. Accordingly, the Financial Crisis Responsibility Fee is intended to recoup the costs of the TARP program as well as discourage excessive risk-taking, as the combination of high levels of risky assets and less stable sources of funding were key contributors to the financial crisis. The structure of this fee would be broadly consistent with the principles agreed to by the G-20 leaders and similar to fees proposed by other countries.

Proposal

The Financial Crisis Responsibility Fee would be assessed on certain liabilities of the largest firms in the financial sector. Specific components of the proposal are described here.

Firms Subject to the Fee: The fee would apply to U.S.-based bank holding companies, thrift holding companies, certain broker-dealers, companies that control certain broker-dealers and insured depository institutions. U.S. companies owning and controlling these types of entities as of January 14, 2010 also would be subject to the fee. Firms with worldwide consolidated assets of less than $50 billion would not be subject to the fee for the period when their assets are below this threshold. U.S. subsidiaries of foreign firms that fall into these categories and that have assets in excess of $50 billion also would be covered.

Base of Fee: The fee would be based on the covered liabilities of a financial firm. Covered liabilities are generally the consolidated risk-weighted assets of a financial firm, less its capital, insured deposits, and certain loans to small business. These would be computed using information filed with the appropriate Federal or State regulators. For insurance companies, certain insurance policy reserves and other policyholder obligations also would be deducted in computing covered liabilities. In addition, adjustments would be provided to prevent avoidance.

Fee Rates: The rate of the fee applied to covered liabilities would be approximately 7.5 basis points. A discount would apply to more stable sources of funding, including long-term liabilities.

Deductibility: The fee would be deductible in computing corporate income tax.

Filing and Payment Requirements: A financial entity subject to the fee would report it on its annual Federal income tax return. Estimated payments of the fee would be made on the same schedule as estimated income tax payments.

The fee would be effective as of the day after December 31, 2012.

REQUIRE ACCRUAL OF INCOME ON FORWARD SALE OF CORPORATE STOCK

Current Law

A corporation generally does not recognize gain or loss on the issuance or repurchase of its own stock. Thus, a corporation does not recognize gain or loss on the forward sale of its own stock. A corporation sells its stock forward by agreeing to issue its stock in the future in exchange for consideration to be paid in the future.

Although a corporation does not recognize gain or loss on the issuance of its own stock, a corporation does recognize interest income upon the current sale of any stock (including its own) for deferred payment.

Reasons for Change

There is little substantive difference between a corporate issuer's current sale of its stock for deferred payment and an issuer's forward sale of the same stock. The only difference between the two transactions is the timing of the stock issuance. In a current sale, the stock is issued at the inception of the transaction, but in a forward sale, the stock is issued at the time the deferred payment is received. In both cases, a portion of the deferred payment economically compensates the corporation for the time value of deferring receipt of the payment. It is inappropriate to treat these two transactions differently.

Proposal

The proposal would require a corporation that enters into a forward contract to issue its stock to treat a portion of the payment on the forward issuance as a payment of interest.

The proposal would be effective for forward contracts entered into after December 31, 2011.

REQUIRE ORDINARY TREATMENT OF INCOME FROM DAY-TO-DAY DEALER ACTIVITIES FOR CERTAIN DEALERS OF EQUITY OPTIONS AND COMMODITIES

Current Law

Under current law, certain dealers treat the income from some of their day-to-day dealer activities as capital gain. This special rule applies to certain transactions in section 1256 contracts by commodities dealers (within the meaning of section 1402(i)(2)(B)), commodities derivatives dealers (within the meaning of section 1221(b)(1)(A)), dealers in securities (within the meaning of section 475(c)(1)), and options dealers (within the meaning of section 1256(g)(8)). Under section 1256, these dealers treat 60 percent of their income (or loss) from their dealer activities in section 1256 contracts as long-term capital gain (or loss) and 40 percent of their income (or loss) from these dealer activities as short-term capital gain (or loss). Dealers in other types of property generally treat the income from their day-to-day dealer activities as ordinary income.

Reasons for Change

There is no reason to treat dealers in commodities, commodities derivatives dealers, dealers in securities, and dealers in options differently from dealers in other types of property. Dealers earn their income from their day-to-day dealer activities, and this income should be taxed at ordinary rates.

Proposal

The proposal would require dealers in commodities, commodities derivatives dealers, dealers in securities, and dealers in options to treat the income from their day-to-day dealer activities in section 1256 contracts as ordinary in character, not capital.

The proposal would be effective for taxable years beginning after the date of enactment.

MODIFY THE DEFINITION OF "CONTROL" FOR PURPOSES OF SECTION 249 OF THE INTERNAL REVENUE CODE

Current Law

In general, if a corporation repurchases a debt instrument that is convertible into its stock, or into stock of a corporation in control of, or controlled by, the corporation, section 249 may disallow or limit the issuer's deduction for a premium paid to repurchase the debt instrument. For this purpose, "control" is determined by reference to section 368(c), which encompasses only direct relationships (e.g., a parent corporation and its wholly-owned, first-tier subsidiary).

Reasons for Change

The definition of "control" in section 249 is unnecessarily restrictive and has allowed the limitation in section 249 to be too easily avoided. Indirect control relationships (e.g., a parent corporation and a second-tier subsidiary) present the same economic identity of interests as direct control relationships and should be treated in a similar manner.

Proposal

The proposal would amend the definition of "control" in section 249(b)(2) to incorporate indirect control relationships of the nature described in section 1563(a)(1).

The proposal would be effective on the date of enactment.

Reinstate Superfund Taxes

REINSTATE SUPERFUND EXCISE TAXES

Current Law

The following Superfund excise taxes were imposed before January 1, 1996:

(1) An excise tax on domestic crude oil and on imported petroleum products at a rate of 9.7 cents per barrel;

(2) An excise tax on listed hazardous chemicals at a rate that varied from 22 cents to $4.87 per ton; and

(3) An excise tax on imported substances that use as materials in their manufacture or production one or more of the hazardous chemicals subject to the excise tax described in (2) above.

Amounts equivalent to the revenues from these taxes were dedicated to the Hazardous Substance Superfund Trust Fund (the Superfund Trust Fund). Amounts in the Superfund Trust Fund are available for expenditures incurred in connection with releases or threats of releases of hazardous substances into the environment under specified provisions of the Comprehensive Environmental Response, Compensation, and Liability Act of 1980 (as amended).

Reasons for Change

The Superfund excise taxes should be reinstated because of the continuing need for funds to remedy damages caused by releases of hazardous substances.

Proposal

The proposal would reinstate the three Superfund excise taxes for periods after December 31, 2011 and before January 1, 2022.

REINSTATE SUPERFUND ENVIRONMENTAL INCOME TAX

Current Law

For taxable years beginning before January 1, 1996, a corporate environmental income tax was imposed at a rate of 0.12 percent on the amount by which the modified alternative minimum taxable income of a corporation exceeded $2 million. Modified alternative minimum taxable income was defined as a corporation's alternative minimum taxable income, determined without regard to the alternative tax net operating loss deduction and the deduction for the corporate environmental income tax.

The tax was dedicated to the Hazardous Substance Superfund Trust Fund (the Superfund Trust Fund). Amounts in the Superfund Trust Fund are available for expenditures incurred in connection with releases or threats of releases of hazardous substances into the environment under specified provisions of the Comprehensive Environmental Response, Compensation, and Liability Act of 1980 (as amended).

Reasons for Change

The corporate environmental income tax should be reinstated because of the continuing need for funds to remedy damages caused by releases of hazardous substances.

Proposal

The proposal would reinstate the corporate environmental income tax for taxable years beginning after December 31, 2011 and before January 1, 2022.

Reform U.S. International Tax System

DEFER DEDUCTION OF INTEREST EXPENSE RELATED TO DEFERRED INCOME

Current Law

Taxpayers generally may deduct ordinary and necessary expenses paid or incurred in carrying on any trade or business. The Internal Revenue Code and the regulations thereunder contain detailed rules regarding allocation and apportionment of expenses for computing taxable income from sources within and without the United States. Under current rules, a U.S. person that incurs interest expense properly allocable and apportioned to foreign-source income may deduct those expenses even if the expenses exceed the taxpayer's gross foreign-source income or if the taxpayer earns no foreign-source income. For example, a U.S. person that incurs debt to acquire stock of a foreign corporation is generally permitted to deduct currently the interest expense from the acquisition indebtedness even if no income is derived currently from such stock. Current law includes provisions that may require a U.S. person to recapture as U.S.-source income the amount by which foreign-source expenses exceed foreign-source income for a taxable year. However, if in a taxable year the U.S. person earns sufficient foreign-source income of the same statutory grouping in which the stock of the foreign corporation is classified, expenses, such as interest expense, properly allocated and apportioned to the stock of the foreign corporation may not be subject to recapture in a subsequent taxable year.

Reasons for Change

The ability to deduct expenses from overseas investments while deferring U.S. tax on the income from the investment may cause U.S. businesses to shift their investments and jobs overseas, harming our domestic economy.

Proposal

The proposal would defer the deduction of interest expense that is properly allocated and apportioned to a taxpayer's foreign-source income that is not currently subject to U.S. tax. For purposes of the proposal, foreign-source income earned by a taxpayer through a branch would be considered currently subject to U.S. tax; thus, the proposal would not apply to interest expense properly allocated and apportioned to such income. Other directly earned foreign source income (for example, royalty income) would be similarly treated.

For purposes of the proposal, the amount of a taxpayer's interest expense that is properly allocated and apportioned to foreign-source income would generally be determined under current Treasury regulations. The Treasury Department, however, will revise existing Treasury regulations and propose such other statutory changes as necessary to prevent inappropriate decreases in the amount of interest expense that is allocated and apportioned to foreign-source income.

Deferred interest expense would be deductible in a subsequent tax year in proportion to the amount of the previously deferred foreign-source income that is subject to U.S. tax during that subsequent tax year. Treasury regulations may modify the manner in which a taxpayer can deduct previously deferred interest expenses in certain cases.

The proposal would be effective for taxable years beginning after December 31, 2011.

DETERMINE THE FOREIGN TAX CREDIT ON A POOLING BASIS

Current Law

Section 901 provides that, subject to certain limitations, a taxpayer may choose to claim a credit against its U.S. income tax liability for income, war profits, and excess profits taxes paid or accrued during the taxable year to any foreign country or any possession of the United States. Under section 902, a domestic corporation is deemed to have paid the foreign taxes paid by certain foreign subsidiaries from which it receives a dividend (the deemed paid foreign tax credit). The foreign tax credit is limited to an amount equal to the pre-credit U.S. tax on the taxpayer's foreign-source income. This foreign tax credit limitation is applied separately to foreign-source income in each of the separate categories described in section 904(d)(1), i.e., the passive category and general category.

Reasons for Change

The purpose of the foreign tax credit is to mitigate the potential for double taxation when U.S. taxpayers are subject to foreign taxes on their foreign-source income. The reduction to two foreign tax credit limitation categories, for passive category income and general category income under the American Jobs Creation Act of 2004, enhanced U.S. taxpayers' ability to reduce the residual U.S. tax on foreign-source income through "cross-crediting."

Proposal

The proposal would require a U.S. taxpayer to determine its deemed paid foreign tax credit on a consolidated basis based on the aggregate foreign taxes and earnings and profits of all of the foreign subsidiaries with respect to which the U.S. taxpayer can claim a deemed paid foreign tax credit (including lower tier subsidiaries described in section 902(b)). The deemed paid foreign tax credit for a taxable year would be determined based on the amount of the consolidated earnings and profits of the foreign subsidiaries repatriated to the U.S. taxpayer in that taxable year. The Secretary would be granted authority to issue any Treasury regulations necessary to carry out the purposes of the proposal.

The proposal would be effective for taxable years beginning after December 31, 2011.

TAX CURRENTLY EXCESS RETURNS ASSOCIATED WITH TRANSFERS OF INTANGIBLES OFFSHORE

Current Law

Section 482 authorizes the Secretary to distribute, apportion, or allocate gross income, deductions, credits, and other allowances between or among two or more organizations, trades, or businesses under common ownership or control whenever "necessary in order to prevent evasion of taxes or clearly to reflect the income of any of such organizations, trades, or businesses." The regulations under section 482 provide that the standard to be applied is that of unrelated persons dealing at arm's length. In the case of transfers of intangible assets, section 482 further provides that the income with respect to the transaction must be commensurate with the income attributable to the transferred intangible assets.

In general, the subpart F rules (sections 951-964) require U.S. shareholders with a 10-percent or greater interest in a controlled foreign corporation (CFC) to include currently in income for U.S. tax purposes their pro rata share of certain income of the CFC (referred to as "subpart F income"), without regard to whether the income is actually distributed to the shareholders. A CFC generally is defined as any foreign corporation if U.S. persons own (directly, indirectly, or constructively) more than 50 percent of the corporation's stock (measured by vote or value), taking into account only those U.S. persons that own at least 10 percent of the corporation's voting stock.

Subpart F income consists of foreign base company income, insurance income, and certain income relating to international boycotts and other proscribed activities. Foreign base company income consists of foreign personal holding company income (which includes passive income such as dividends, interest, rents, royalties, and annuities) and other categories of income from business operations, including foreign base company sales income, foreign base company services income, and foreign base company oil-related income.

A foreign tax credit is generally available for foreign income taxes paid by a CFC to the extent that the CFC's income is taxed to a U.S. shareholder under subpart F, subject to the limitations set forth in section 904.

Reasons for Change

The potential tax savings from transactions between related parties, especially with regard to transfers of intangible assets to low-taxed affiliates, puts significant pressure on the enforcement and effective application of transfer pricing rules. There is evidence indicating that income shifting through transfers of intangibles to low-taxed affiliates has resulted in a significant erosion of the U.S. tax base. Expanding subpart F to include excess income from intangibles transferred to low-taxed affiliates will reduce the incentive for taxpayers to engage in these transactions.

Proposal

The proposal would provide that if a U.S. person transfers (directly or indirectly) an intangible from the United States to a related CFC (a "covered intangible"), then certain excess income from transactions connected with or benefitting from the covered intangible would be treated as subpart F income if the income is subject to a low foreign effective tax rate. For this purpose, excess intangible income would be defined as the excess of gross income from transactions connected with or benefitting from such covered intangible over the costs (excluding interest and taxes) properly allocated and apportioned to this income increased by a percentage mark-up. For purposes of this proposal, the transfer of an intangible includes by sale, lease, license, or through any shared risk or development agreement (including any cost sharing arrangement)). This subpart F income will be a separate category of income for purposes of determining the taxpayer's foreign tax credit limitation under section 904.

The proposal would be effective for transactions in taxable years beginning after December 31, 2011.

LIMIT SHIFTING OF INCOME THROUGH INTANGIBLE PROPERTY TRANSFERS

Current Law

Section 482 authorizes the Secretary to distribute, apportion, or allocate gross income, deductions, credits, and other allowances between or among two or more organizations, trades, or businesses under common ownership or control whenever "necessary in order to prevent evasion of taxes or clearly to reflect the income of any of such organizations, trades, or businesses." Section 482 also provides that in the case of transfers of intangible assets, the income with respect to the transaction must be commensurate with the income attributable to the transferred intangible assets. Further, under section 367(d), if a U.S. person transfers intangible property (as defined in section 936(h)(3)(B)) to a foreign corporation in certain nonrecognition transactions, the U.S. person is treated as selling the intangible property for a series of payments contingent on the productivity, use, or disposition of the property that are commensurate with the transferee's income from the property. The payments generally continue annually over the useful life of the property.

Reasons for Change

Controversy often arises concerning the value of intangible property transferred between related persons and the scope of the intangible property subject to sections 482 and 367(d). This lack of clarity may result in the inappropriate avoidance of U.S. tax and misuse of the rules applicable to transfers of intangible property to foreign persons.

Proposal

The proposal would clarify the definition of intangible property for purposes of sections 367(d) and 482 to include workforce in place, goodwill and going concern value. The proposal also would clarify that where multiple intangible properties are transferred, the Commissioner may value the intangible properties on an aggregate basis where that achieves a more reliable result. In addition, the proposal would clarify that the Commissioner may value intangible property taking into consideration the prices or profits that the controlled taxpayer could have realized by choosing a realistic alternative to the controlled transaction undertaken.

The proposal would be effective for taxable years beginning after December 31, 2011.

DISALLOW THE DEDUCTION FOR NON-TAXED REINSURANCE PREMIUMS PAID TO AFFILIATES

Current Law

Insurance companies are generally allowed a deduction for premiums paid for reinsurance. If the reinsurance transaction results in a transfer of reserves and reserve assets to the reinsurer, potential tax liability for earnings on those assets is generally shifted to the reinsurer as well. While insurance income of a controlled foreign corporation is generally subject to current U.S. taxation, insurance income of a foreign-owned foreign company that is not engaged in a trade or business in the United States is not subject to U.S. income tax. Reinsurance policies issued by foreign reinsurers with respect to U.S. risks are generally subject to an excise tax equal to one percent of the premiums paid, unless waived by treaty.

Reasons for Change

Reinsurance transactions with affiliates that are not subject to U.S. federal income tax on insurance income can result in substantial U.S. tax advantages over similar transactions with entities that are subject to tax in the United States. The excise tax on reinsurance policies issued by foreign reinsurers is not always sufficient to offset this tax advantage. These tax advantages create an inappropriate incentive for foreign-owned domestic insurance companies to reinsure U.S. risks with foreign affiliates.

Proposal

The proposal would (1) deny an insurance company a deduction for reinsurance premiums paid to affiliated foreign reinsurance companies to the extent that the foreign reinsurer (or its parent company) is not subject to U.S. income tax with respect to the premiums received; and (2) would exclude from the insurance company's income (in the same proportion that the premium deduction was denied) any ceding commissions received or reinsurance recovered with respect to reinsurance policies for which a premium deduction is wholly or partially denied.

A foreign corporation that is paid a premium from an affiliate that would otherwise be denied a deduction under this proposal would be permitted to elect to treat those premiums and the associated investment income as income effectively connected with the conduct of a trade or business in the United States and attributable to a permanent establishment for tax treaty purposes. For foreign tax credit purposes, reinsurance income treated as effectively connected under this rule would be treated as foreign source income and would be placed into a separate category within section 904.

The provision is effective for policies issued in taxable years beginning after December 31, 2011.

LIMIT EARNINGS STRIPPING BY EXPATRIATED ENTITIES

Current Law

Section 163(j) limits the deductibility of certain interest paid by a corporation to related persons. The limitation applies to a corporation that fails a debt-to-equity safe harbor (greater than 1.5 to 1) and that has net interest expense in excess of 50 percent of adjusted taxable income (generally computed by adding back net interest expense, depreciation, amortization and depletion, any net operating loss deduction, and any deduction for domestic production activities under section 199). Disallowed interest expense may be carried forward indefinitely for deduction in a subsequent year. In addition, the corporation's excess limitation for a tax year (i.e., the amount by which 50 percent of adjusted taxable income exceeds net interest expense) may be carried forward to the three subsequent tax years.

Section 7874 provides special rules for expatriated entities and the acquiring foreign corporations. The rules apply to certain defined transactions in which a U.S. parent company (the expatriated entity) is essentially replaced with a foreign parent (the surrogate foreign corporation). The tax treatment of an expatriated entity and a surrogate foreign corporation varies depending on the extent of continuity of shareholder ownership following the transaction. The surrogate foreign corporation is treated as a domestic corporation for all purposes of the Code if shareholder ownership continuity is at least 80 percent (by vote or value). If shareholder ownership continuity is at least 60 percent, but less than 80 percent, the surrogate foreign corporation is treated as a foreign corporation but certain tax consequences apply, including that any applicable corporate-level income or gain required to be recognized by the expatriated entity generally cannot be offset by tax attributes. Section 7874 generally applies to transactions occurring on or after March 4, 2003.

Reasons for Change

Under current law, opportunities are available to reduce inappropriately the U.S. tax on income earned from U.S. operations through the use of foreign related-party debt. In its 2007 study of earnings stripping, the Treasury Department found strong evidence of the use of such techniques by expatriated entities. Consequently, amending the rules of section 163(j) for expatriated entities is necessary to prevent these inappropriate income-reduction opportunities.

Proposal

The proposal would revise section 163(j) to tighten the limitation on the deductibility of interest paid by an expatriated entity to related persons. The current law debt-to-equity safe harbor would be eliminated. The 50 percent adjusted taxable income threshold for the limitation would be reduced to 25 percent. The carryforward for disallowed interest would be limited to ten years and the carryforward of excess limitation would be eliminated.

An expatriated entity would be defined by applying the rules of section 7874 and the regulations thereunder as if section 7874 were applicable for taxable years beginning after July 10, 1989. This special rule would not apply, however, if the surrogate foreign corporation is treated as a domestic corporation under section 7874.

The proposal would be effective for taxable years beginning after December 31, 2011.

MODIFY THE TAX RULES FOR DUAL CAPACITY TAXPAYERS

Current Law

Section 901 provides that, subject to certain limitations, a taxpayer may choose to claim a credit against its U.S. income tax liability for income, war profits, and excess profits taxes paid or accrued during the taxable year to any foreign country or any possession of the United States. To be a creditable tax, a foreign levy must be substantially equivalent to an income tax under United States tax principles, regardless of the label attached to the levy under law. Under current Treasury regulations, a foreign levy is a tax if it is a compulsory payment under the authority of a foreign government to levy taxes and is not compensation for a specific economic benefit provided by the foreign country. Taxpayers that are subject to a foreign levy and that also receive a specific economic benefit from the levying country (dual capacity taxpayers) may not credit the portion of the foreign levy paid for the specific economic benefit. The current Treasury regulations provide that, if a foreign country has a generally-imposed income tax, the dual capacity taxpayer may treat as a creditable tax the portion of the levy that application of the generally imposed income tax would yield (provided that the levy otherwise constitutes an income tax or an in lieu of tax). The balance of the levy is treated as compensation for the specific economic benefit. If the foreign country does not generally impose an income tax, the portion of the payment that does not exceed the applicable federal tax rate applied to net income is treated as a creditable tax. A foreign tax is treated as generally imposed even if it applies only to persons who are not residents or nationals of that country.

There is no separate section 904 foreign tax credit limitation category for oil and gas income. However, under section 907, the amount of creditable foreign taxes imposed on foreign oil and gas income is limited in any year to the applicable U.S. tax on that income.

Reasons for Change

The purpose of the foreign tax credit is to mitigate double taxation of income by the United States and a foreign country. When a payment is made to a foreign country in exchange for a specific economic benefit, there is no double taxation. Current law recognizes the distinction between a payment of creditable taxes and a payment in exchange for a specific economic benefit but fails to achieve the appropriate split between the two when a single payment is made in a case where, for example, a foreign country imposes a levy only on oil and gas income, or imposes a higher levy on oil and gas income as compared to other income.

Proposal

The proposal would allow a dual capacity taxpayer to treat as a creditable tax the portion of a foreign levy that does not exceed the foreign levy that the taxpayer would pay if it were not a dual-capacity taxpayer. The proposal would replace the current regulatory provisions, including the safe harbor, that apply to determine the amount of a foreign levy paid by a dual-capacity taxpayer that qualifies as a creditable tax. The proposal also would convert the special foreign tax credit limitation rules of section 907 into a separate category within section 904 for foreign oil and gas income. The proposal would yield to United States treaty obligations to the extent that they allow a credit for taxes paid or accrued on certain oil or gas income.

The proposal would be effective for taxable years beginning after December 31, 2011.

Reform Treatment of Insurance Companies and Products

MODIFY RULES THAT APPLY TO SALES OF LIFE INSURANCE CONTRACTS

Current Law

The seller of a life insurance contract generally must report as taxable income the difference between the amount received from the buyer and the adjusted basis in the contract, unless the buyer is a viatical settlement provider and the insured person is terminally or chronically ill.

Under a transfer-for-value rule, the buyer of a previously-issued life insurance contract who subsequently receives a death benefit generally is subject to tax on the difference between the death benefit received and the sum of the amount paid for the contract and premiums subsequently paid by the buyer. This rule does not apply if the buyer's basis is determined in whole or in part by reference to the seller's basis, nor does the rule apply if the buyer is the insured, a partner of the insured, a partnership in which the insured is a partner, or a corporation in which the insured is a shareholder or officer.

Persons engaged in a trade or business that make payments of premiums, compensations, remunerations, other fixed or determinable gains, profits and income, or certain other types of payments in the course of that trade or business to another person generally are required to report such payments of $600 or more to the Internal Revenue Service (IRS). However, reporting may not be required in some circumstances involving the purchase of a life insurance contract.

Reasons for Change

Recent years have seen a significant increase in the number and size of life settlement transactions, wherein individuals sell previously-issued life insurance contracts to investors. Compliance is sometimes hampered by a lack of information reporting. In addition, the current law exceptions to the transfer-for-value rule may give investors the ability to structure a transaction to avoid paying tax on the profit when the insured person dies.

Proposal

The proposal would require a person or entity who purchases an interest in an existing life insurance contract with a death benefit equal to or exceeding $500,000 to report the purchase price, the buyer's and seller's taxpayer identification numbers (TINs), and the issuer and policy number to the IRS, to the insurance company that issued the policy, and to the seller.

The proposal also would modify the transfer-for-value rule to ensure that exceptions to that rule would not apply to buyers of policies. Upon the payment of any policy benefits to the buyer, the insurance company would be required to report the gross benefit payment, the buyer's TIN, and the insurance company's estimate of the buyer's basis to the IRS and to the payee.

The proposal would apply to sales or assignment of interests in life insurance policies and payments of death benefits in taxable years beginning after December 31, 2011.

51

MODIFY DIVIDENDS-RECEIVED DEDUCTION (DRD) FOR LIFE INSURANCE COMPANY SEPARATE ACCOUNTS

Current Law

Corporate taxpayers may generally qualify for a DRD with regard to dividends received from other domestic corporations, in order to prevent or limit taxable inclusion of the same income by more than one corporation. No DRD is allowed, however, in respect of any dividend on any share of stock (1) to the extent the taxpayer is under an obligation to make related payments with respect to positions in substantially similar or related property, or (2) that is held by the taxpayer for 45 days or less during the 91-day period beginning on the date that is 45 days before the share becomes ex-dividend with respect to the dividend. For this purpose, the taxpayer's holding period is reduced for any period in which the taxpayer has diminished its risk of loss by holding one or more positions with respect to substantially similar or related property.

In the case of a life insurance company, the DRD is permitted only with regard to the "company's share" of dividends received, reflecting the fact that some portion of the company's dividend income is used to fund tax-deductible reserves for its obligations to policyholders. Likewise, the net increase or net decrease in reserves is computed by reducing the ending balance of the reserve items by the policyholders' share of tax-exempt interest. The regime for computing the company's share and policyholders' share of net investment income is sometimes referred to as proration.

The policyholders' share equals 100 percent less the company's share, whereas the latter is equal to the company's share of net investment income divided by net investment income. The company's share of net investment income is the excess, if any, of net investment income over certain amounts, including "required interest," that are set aside to satisfy obligations to policyholders. Required interest with regard to an account is calculated by multiplying a specified account earnings rate by the mean of the reserves with regard to the account for the taxable year.

A life insurance company's separate account assets, liabilities, and income are segregated from those of the company's general account in order to support variable life insurance and variable annuity contracts. A company's share and policyholders' share are computed for the company's general account and separately for each separate account.

Reasons for Change

The proration methodology currently used by some taxpayers may produce a company's share that greatly exceeds the company's economic interest in the net investment income earned by its separate account assets, generating controversy between life insurance companies and the Internal Revenue Service. The purposes of the proration regime would be better served, and life insurance companies would be treated more like other taxpayers with a diminished risk of loss in stock or an obligation to make related payments with respect to dividends, if the company's share bore a more direct relationship to the company's actual economic interest in the account.

Proposal

The proposal would repeal the existing regime for prorating investment income between the "company's share" and the "policyholders' share." The general account DRD, tax-exempt interest, and increases in certain policy cash values of a life insurance company would instead be subject to a fixed 15 percent proration in a manner similar to that which applies under current law to non-life insurance companies. The limitations on DRD that apply to other corporate taxpayers would be expanded to apply explicitly to life insurance company separate account dividends in the same proportion as the mean of reserves bears to the mean of total assets of the account. The proposal would thus put the company's general account DRD on a similar footing to that of a non-life company, and would put its separate account DRD on a similar footing to that of any other taxpayer with a diminished risk of loss in stock that it owns, or with an obligation to make related payments with regard to dividends.

The proposal would be effective for taxable years beginning after December 31, 2011.

EXPAND PRO RATA INTEREST EXPENSE DISALLOWANCE FOR CORPORATE-OWED LIFE INSURANCE

Current Law

In general, no Federal income tax is imposed on a policyholder with respect to the earnings credited under a life insurance or endowment contract, and Federal income tax generally is deferred with respect to earnings under an annuity contract (unless the annuity contract is owned by a person other than a natural person). In addition, amounts received under a life insurance contract by reason of the death of the insured generally are excluded from gross income of the recipient.

Interest on policy loans or other indebtedness with respect to life insurance, endowment or annuity contracts generally is not deductible, unless the insurance contract insures the life of a key person of the business. A key person includes a 20-percent owner of the business, as well as a limited number of the business' officers or employees. However, this interest disallowance rule applies to businesses only to the extent that the indebtedness can be traced to a life insurance, endowment or annuity contract.

In addition, the interest deductions of a business other than an insurance company are reduced to the extent the interest is allocable to unborrowed policy cash values based on a statutory formula. An exception to the pro rata interest disallowance applies with respect to contracts that cover individuals who are officers, directors, employees, or 20-percent owners of the taxpayer. In the case of both life and non-life insurance companies, special proration rules similarly require adjustments to prevent or limit the funding of tax-deductible reserve increases with tax preferred income, including earnings credited under life insurance, endowment and annuity contracts that would be subject to the pro rata interest disallowance rule if owned by a non-insurance company.

Reasons for Change

Leveraged businesses can fund deductible interest expenses with tax-exempt or tax-deferred income credited under life insurance, endowment or annuity contracts insuring certain types of individuals. For example, these businesses frequently invest in investment-oriented insurance policies covering the lives of their employees, officers, directors or owners. These entities generally do not take out policy loans or other indebtedness that is secured or otherwise traceable to the insurance contracts. Instead, they borrow from depositors or other lenders, or issue bonds. Similar tax arbitrage benefits result when insurance companies invest in certain insurance contracts that cover the lives of their employees, officers, directors or 20-percent shareholders and fund deductible reserves with tax-exempt or tax-deferred income.

Proposal

The proposal would repeal the exception from the pro rata interest expense disallowance rule for contracts covering employees, officers or directors, other than 20-percent owners of a business that is the owner or beneficiary of the contracts.

The proposal would apply to contracts issued after December 31, 2011, in taxable years ending after that date. For this purpose, any material increase in the death benefit or other material change in the contract would be treated as a new contract except that in the case of a master contract, the addition of covered lives would be treated as a new contract only with respect to the additional covered lives.

Miscellaneous Changes

INCREASE THE OIL SPILL LIABILITY TRUST FUND FINANCING RATE BY ONE CENT

Current Law

An excise tax is imposed on domestic crude oil and on imported petroleum products at a rate of 8 cents per barrel (9 cents per barrel after December 31, 2016). The tax is deposited in the Oil Spill Liability Trust Fund to pay costs associated with oil removal and damages resulting from oil spills, as well as to provide annual funding to certain agencies for a wide range of oil pollution prevention and response programs, including research and development. In an oil spill, the fund makes it possible for the Federal government to pay for removal costs up front, and then seek full reimbursement from the responsible parties.

Reasons for Change

The Deepwater Horizon oil spill was the worst oil spill in American history, releasing nearly 5 million barrels of oil into the Gulf of Mexico, and led to the nation's largest oil spill response. The magnitude of the Federal response reinforced the importance of the Oil Spill Liability Trust Fund and the need to maintain a sufficient balance, particularly in order to accommodate spills of national significance.

Proposal

The proposal would increase the rate of the Oil Spill Liability Trust Fund tax to 9 cents per barrel for periods after December 31, 2011, and to 10 cents per barrel for periods after December 31, 2016.

MAKE UNEMPLOYMENT INSURANCE SURTAX PERMANENT

Current Law

The Federal Unemployment Tax Act (FUTA) currently imposes a Federal payroll tax on employers of 6.2 percent of the first $7,000 paid annually to each employee. The tax funds a portion of the Federal/State unemployment benefits system. This 6.2 percent rate includes a temporary surtax of 0.2 percent (discussed below). States also impose an unemployment tax on employers. Employers in States that meet certain Federal requirements are allowed a credit for State unemployment taxes of up to 5.4 percent, making the minimum net Federal tax rate 0.8 percent. Generally, Federal and State unemployment taxes are collected quarterly and deposited in Federal trust fund accounts.

In 1976, Congress passed a temporary surtax of 0.2 percent of taxable wages to be added to the permanent FUTA tax rate. Thus, the current 0.8 percent net FUTA tax rate has two components: a permanent tax rate of 0.6 percent and a temporary surtax rate of 0.2 percent. The surtax has been extended several times, most recently through June 30, 2011.

Reasons for Change

Extending the surtax will support the continued solvency of the Federal unemployment trust funds.

Proposal

The proposal would make the 0.2 percent surtax permanent.

The proposal would be effective as of the date of enactment.

PROVIDE SHORT-TERM TAX RELIEF TO EMPLOYERS AND EXPAND FEDERAL UNEMPLOYMENT TAX ACT (FUTA) BASE

Current Law

The FUTA currently imposes a Federal payroll tax on employers of 6.2 percent of the first $7,000 paid annually to each employee. Generally, these funds support the administrative costs of the unemployment insurance (UI) benefits system. Employers in States that meet certain Federal requirements are allowed a credit against FUTA taxes of up to 5.4 percent, making the minimum net Federal rate 0.8 percent. States that become non-compliant experience a reduction in FUTA credit, causing employers to face a higher Federal UI tax.

Each State also imposes an unemployment insurance tax on employers to fund its State UI trust fund. State UI trust funds are used to pay unemployment benefits. When State trust funds are exhausted, States borrow from the Federal UI trust fund to pay for unemployment benefits. States that borrow from the Federal UI trust fund are required to pay back the borrowed amount including interest. This debt is partly repaid by increases in the Federal UI tax (reductions in the credit) on employers in these States.

Reasons for Change

In aggregate, States entered this recession with extremely low levels of reserves in their trust funds. Partly because of this, States have accrued large amounts of debt to the Federal UI trust fund. Employers in indebted States face immediate tax increases to repay these debts. These tax increases discourage job creation at a time when growth is needed. At the same time, many States do not have a long-term plan to restore solvency to their trust funds. Short-term relief from State debt burdens coupled with longer-term increases in States' minimum taxable wage base will encourage economic growth and lead many States to repay the debts they owe, restoring solvency to the UI system.

Proposal

The proposal would provide short-term relief to employers by suspending interest payments on State UI debt and suspending the FUTA credit reduction for employers in borrowing States in 2011 and 2012. The proposal would also raise the FUTA wage base to $15,000 per worker paid annually in 2014, index the wage base to wage growth for subsequent years, and reduce the net Federal UI tax from 0.8 percent (after the proposed permanent extension of the FUTA surtax) to 0.38 percent. States with wage bases below $15,000 would need to conform to the new FUTA base. States would maintain the ability to set their own tax rates, as under current law.

The proposal would be effective upon the date of enactment.

REPEAL LAST-IN, FIRST-OUT (LIFO) METHOD OF ACCOUNTING FOR INVENTORIES

Current Law

A taxpayer with inventory may determine the value of its inventory and its cost of goods sold using a number of different methods. The most prevalent method is the first-in, first-out (FIFO) method, which matches current sales with the costs of the earliest acquired (or manufactured) inventory items. As an alternative, a taxpayer may elect to use the LIFO method, which treats the most recently acquired (or manufactured) goods as having been sold during the year. The LIFO method can provide a tax benefit for a taxpayer facing rising inventory costs, since the cost of goods sold under this method is based on more recent, higher inventory values, resulting in lower taxable income. If inventory levels fall during the year, however, a LIFO taxpayer must include lower-cost LIFO inventory values (reflecting one or more prior-year inventory accumulations) in the cost of goods sold, and its taxable income will be correspondingly higher. To be eligible to elect LIFO for tax purposes, a taxpayer must use LIFO for financial accounting purposes.

Reasons for Change

The repeal of the LIFO method would eliminate a tax deferral opportunity available to taxpayers that hold inventories, the costs of which increase over time. In addition, LIFO repeal would simplify the Code by removing a complex and burdensome accounting method that has been the source of controversy between taxpayers and the Internal Revenue Service.

International Financial Reporting Standards do not permit the use of the LIFO method, and their adoption by the Securities and Exchange Commission would cause violations of the current LIFO book/tax conformity requirement. Repealing LIFO would remove this possible impediment to the implementation of these standards in the United States.

Proposal

The proposal would not allow the use of the LIFO inventory accounting method for Federal income tax purposes. Taxpayers that currently use the LIFO method would be required to write up their beginning LIFO inventory to its FIFO value in the first taxable year beginning after December 31, 2012. However, this one-time increase in gross income would be taken into account ratably over ten years, beginning with the first taxable year beginning after December 31, 2012.

REPEAL GAIN LIMITATION FOR DIVIDENDS RECEIVED IN REORGANIZATION EXCHANGES

Current Law

Under section 356(a)(1), if as part of a reorganization transaction an exchanging shareholder receives in exchange for its stock of the target corporation both stock and property that cannot be received without the recognition of gain (often referred to as "boot"), the exchanging shareholder is required to recognize gain equal to the lesser of the gain realized in the exchange or the amount of boot received (commonly referred to as the "boot within gain" limitation). Further, under section 356(a)(2), if the exchange has the effect of the distribution of a dividend, then all or part of the gain recognized by the exchanging shareholder is treated as a dividend to the extent of the shareholder's ratable share of the corporation's earnings and profits. The remainder of the gain (if any) is treated as gain from the exchange of property.

Reasons for Change

There is not a significant policy reason to vary the treatment of a distribution that otherwise qualifies as a dividend by reference to whether it is received in the normal course of a corporation's operations or is instead received as part of a reorganization exchange. Thus, repealing the boot-within-gain limitation for an exchange that has the effect of the distribution of a dividend will provide more uniform treatment for dividends that is less dependent on context. Moreover, in cross-border reorganizations, the boot-within-gain limitation can permit U.S. shareholders to repatriate previously-untaxed earnings and profits of foreign subsidiaries with minimal U.S. tax consequences. For example, if the exchanging shareholder's stock in the target corporation has little or no built-in gain at the time of the exchange, the shareholder will recognize minimal gain even if the exchange has the effect of the distribution of a dividend and/or a significant amount (or all) of the consideration received in the exchange is boot. This result applies even if the corporation has previously untaxed earnings and profits equal to or greater than the boot. This result is inconsistent with the principle that previously untaxed earnings and profits of a foreign subsidiary should be subject to U.S. tax upon repatriation.

Proposal

The proposal would repeal the boot-within-gain limitation of current law in the case of any reorganization transaction if the exchange has the effect of the distribution of a dividend, as determined under section 356(a)(2).

The proposal would be effective for taxable years beginning after December 31, 2011.

TAX CARRIED (PROFITS) INTERESTS IN INVESTMENT PARTNERSHIPS AS ORDINARY INCOME

Current Law

A partnership is not subject to Federal income tax. Instead, an item of income or loss of the partnership retains its character and flows through to the partners, who must include such item on their tax returns. Generally, certain partners receive partnership interests in exchange for contributions of cash and/or property, while certain partners (not necessarily other partners) receive partnership interests, typically interests in future profits ("profits interests" or "carried interests"), in exchange for services. Accordingly, if and to the extent a partnership recognizes long-term capital gain, the partners, including partners who provide services, will reflect their shares of such gain on their tax returns as long-term capital gain. If the partner is an individual, such gain would be taxed at the reduced rates for long-term capital gains. Gain recognized on the sale of a partnership interest, whether it was received in exchange for property, cash or services, is generally treated as capital gain.

Under current law, income attributable to a profits interest of a general partner is generally subject to self-employment tax, except to the extent the partnership generates types of income that are excluded from self-employment taxes, e.g., capital gains, certain interest, and dividends.

Reasons for Change

Although profits interests are structured as partnership interests, the income allocable to such interests is received in connection with the performance of services. A service provider's share of the income of a partnership attributable to a carried interest should be taxed as ordinary income and subject to self-employment tax because such income is derived from the performance of services. By allowing service partners to receive capital gains treatment on labor income without limit, the current system creates an unfair and inefficient tax preference. The recent explosion of activity among large private equity firms and hedge funds has increased the breadth and cost of this tax preference, with some of the highest-income Americans benefiting from the preferential treatment.

Proposal

The proposal would tax as ordinary income a partner's share of income on an "investment services partnership interest" (ISPI) in an investment partnership, regardless of the character of the income at the partnership level. Accordingly, such income would not be eligible for the reduced rates that apply to long-term capital gains. In addition, the proposal would require the partner to pay self-employment taxes on such income. Gain recognized on the sale of an ISPI would generally be taxed as ordinary income, not as capital gain.

An ISPI is a carried interest in an investment partnership that is held by a person who provides services to the partnership. A partnership is an investment partnership if the majority of its assets are investment-type assets (certain securities, real estate, interests in partnerships, commodities, cash or cash equivalents, or derivative contracts with respect to those assets), but only if over half of the partnership's contributed capital is from partners in whose hands the interests constitute property held for the production of income. To the extent that the partner who holds an ISPI contributes "invested capital" and the partnership reasonably allocates its income and loss between such invested capital and the remaining interest, income attributable to the invested capital would not be recharacterized. Similarly, the portion of any gain recognized on the sale of an ISPI that is attributable to the invested capital would be treated as capital gain. "Invested capital" is defined as money or other property contributed to the partnership. However, contributed capital that is attributable to the proceeds of any loan or other advance made or guaranteed by any partner or the partnership is not treated as "invested capital."

Also, any person who performs services for an entity and holds a "disqualified interest" in the entity is subject to tax at rates applicable to ordinary income on any income or gain received with respect to the interest. A "disqualified interest" is defined as convertible or contingent debt, an option, or any derivative instrument with respect to the entity (but does not include a partnership interest or stock in certain taxable corporations). This is an anti-abuse rule designed to prevent the avoidance of the proposal through the use of compensatory arrangements other than partnership interests. Other anti-abuse rules may be necessary.

The proposal is not intended to adversely affect qualification of a real estate investment trust owning a carried interest in a real estate partnership.

The proposal would be effective for taxable years beginning after December 31, 2011.

DENY DEDUCTION FOR PUNITIVE DAMAGES

Current Law

No deduction is allowed for a fine or similar penalty paid to a government for the violation of any law. If a taxpayer is convicted of a violation of the antitrust laws, or the taxpayer's plea of guilty or nolo contendere to such a violation is entered or accepted in a criminal proceeding, no deduction is allowed for two-thirds of any amount paid or incurred on a judgment or in settlement of a civil suit brought under section 4 of the Clayton Antitrust Act on account of such or any related antitrust violation. Where neither of these two provisions is applicable, a deduction is allowed for damages paid or incurred as ordinary and necessary expenses in carrying on any trade or business, regardless of whether such damages are compensatory or punitive.

Reasons for Change

The deductibility of punitive damage payments undermines the role of such damages in discouraging and penalizing certain undesirable actions or activities.

Proposal

The proposal would not allow a deduction for punitive damages paid or incurred by the taxpayer, whether upon a judgment or in settlement of a claim. Where the liability for punitive damages is covered by insurance, such damages paid or incurred by the insurer would be included in the gross income of the insured person. The insurer would be required to report such payments to the insured person and to the Internal Revenue Service.

The proposal would apply to damages paid or incurred after December 31, 2012.

REPEAL LOWER-OF-COST-OR-MARKET (LCM) INVENTORY ACCOUNTING METHOD

Current Law

Taxpayers required to maintain inventories are permitted to use a variety of methods to determine the cost of their ending inventories, including methods such as the last-in, first-out (LIFO) method, the first-in, first-out method, and the retail method. Taxpayers not using a LIFO method may: (1) write down the carrying values of their inventories by applying the LCM method instead of the cost method, and (2) write down the cost of "subnormal" goods (i.e., those that are unsalable at normal prices or unusable in the normal way because of damage, imperfection or other similar causes).

Reasons for Change

The allowance of inventory write-downs under the LCM and subnormal goods provisions is an exception from the realization principle, and is essentially a one-way mark-to-market regime that understates taxable income. Thus, a taxpayer is able to obtain a larger cost-of-goods-sold deduction by writing down an item of inventory if its replacement cost falls below historical cost, but need not increase an item's inventory value if its replacement cost increases above historical cost. This asymmetric treatment is unwarranted. Also, the market value used under LCM for tax purposes generally is the replacement or reproduction cost of an item of inventory, not the item's net realizable value, as is required under generally accepted financial accounting rules. While the operation of the retail method is technically symmetric, it also allows retailers to obtain deductions for write-downs below inventory cost because of normal and anticipated declines in retail prices.

Proposal

The proposal would statutorily prohibit the use of the LCM and subnormal goods methods. Appropriate wash-sale rules also would be included to prevent taxpayers from circumventing the prohibition. The proposal would result in a change in the method of accounting for inventories for taxpayers currently using the LCM and subnormal goods methods, and any resulting section 481(a) adjustment generally would be included in income ratably over a four-year period beginning with the year of change.

The proposal would be effective for taxable years beginning after December 31, 2012.

ELIMINATE FOSSIL-FUEL PREFERENCES

Eliminate Oil and Gas Preferences

REPEAL ENHANCED OIL RECOVERY (EOR) CREDIT

Current Law

The general business credit includes a 15-percent credit for eligible costs attributable to EOR projects. If the credit is claimed with respect to eligible costs, the taxpayer's deduction (or basis increase) with respect to those costs is reduced by the amount of the credit. Eligible costs include the cost of constructing a gas treatment plant to prepare Alaska natural gas for pipeline transportation and any of the following costs with respect to a qualified EOR project: (1) the cost of depreciable or amortizable tangible property that is an integral part of the project; (2) intangible drilling and development costs (IDCs) that the taxpayer can elect to deduct; and (3) deductible tertiary injectant costs. A qualified EOR project must be located in the United States and must involve the application of one or more of nine listed tertiary recovery methods that can reasonably be expected to result in more than an insignificant increase in the amount of crude oil which ultimately will be recovered. The allowable credit is phased out over a $6 range for a taxable year if the annual average unregulated wellhead price per barrel of domestic crude oil during the calendar year preceding the calendar year in which the taxable year begins (the reference price) exceeds an inflation adjusted threshold. The credit was completely phased out for taxable years beginning in 2010, because the reference price ($56.39) exceeded the inflation adjusted threshold ($42.57) by more than $6.

Reasons for Change

The President agreed at the G-20 Summit in Pittsburgh to phase out subsidies for fossil fuels so that the United States can transition to a 21st-century energy economy. The credit, like other oil and gas preferences the Administration proposes to repeal, distorts markets by encouraging more investment in the oil and gas industry than would occur under a neutral system. This market distortion is detrimental to long-term energy security and is also inconsistent with the Administration's policy of supporting a clean energy economy, reducing our reliance on oil, and cutting carbon pollution. Moreover, the credit must ultimately be financed with taxes that result in underinvestment in other, potentially more productive, areas of the economy.

Proposal

The proposal would repeal the investment tax credit for enhanced oil recovery projects for taxable years beginning after December 31, 2011.

REPEAL CREDIT FOR OIL AND GAS PRODUCED FROM MARGINAL WELLS

Current Law

The general business credit includes a credit for crude oil and natural gas produced from marginal wells. The credit rate is $3.00 per barrel of oil and 50 cents per 1,000 cubic feet of natural gas for taxable years beginning in 2005 and is adjusted for inflation in taxable years beginning after 2005. The credit is available for production from wells that produce oil and gas qualifying as marginal production for purposes of the percentage depletion rules or that have average daily production of not more than 25 barrel-of-oil equivalents and produce at least 95 percent water. The credit per well is limited to 1,095 barrels of oil or barrel-of-oil equivalents per year. The credit rate for crude oil is phased out for a taxable year if the annual average unregulated wellhead price per barrel of domestic crude oil during the calendar year preceding the calendar year in which the taxable year begins (the reference price) exceeds the applicable threshold. The phase-out range and the applicable threshold at which phase-out begins are $3.00 and $15.00 for taxable years beginning in 2005 and are adjusted for inflation in taxable years beginning after 2005. The credit rate for natural gas is similarly phased out for a taxable year if the annual average wellhead price for domestic natural gas exceeds the applicable threshold. The phase-out range and the applicable threshold at which phase-out begins are 33 cents and $1.67 for taxable years beginning in 2005 and are adjusted for inflation in taxable years beginning after 2005. The credit has been completely phased out for all taxable years since its enactment. The marginal well credit can be carried back up to five years unlike other components of the general business credit, which can be carried back only one year.

Reasons for Change

The President agreed at the G-20 Summit in Pittsburgh to phase out subsidies for fossil fuels so that the United States can transition to a 21st-century energy economy. The credit, like other oil and gas preferences the Administration proposes to repeal, distorts markets by encouraging more investment in the oil and gas industry than would occur under a neutral system. This market distortion is detrimental to long-term energy security and is also inconsistent with the Administration's policy of supporting a clean energy economy, reducing our reliance on oil, and cutting carbon pollution. Moreover, the credit must ultimately be financed with taxes that result in underinvestment in other, potentially more productive, areas of the economy.

Proposal

The proposal would repeal the production tax credit for oil and gas from marginal wells for production in taxable years beginning after December 31, 2011.

REPEAL EXPENSING OF INTANGIBLE DRILLING COSTS (IDCS)

Current Law

In general, costs that benefit future periods must be capitalized and recovered over such periods for income tax purposes, rather than being expensed in the period the costs are incurred. In addition, the uniform capitalization rules require certain direct and indirect costs allocable to property to be included in inventory or capitalized as part of the basis of such property. In general, the uniform capitalization rules apply to real and tangible personal property produced by the taxpayer or acquired for resale.

Special rules apply to IDCs. IDCs include all expenditures made by an operator for wages, fuel, repairs, hauling, supplies, and other expenses incident to and necessary for the drilling of wells and the preparation of wells for the production of oil and gas. In addition, IDCs include the cost to operators of any drilling or development work (excluding amounts payable only out of production or gross or net proceeds from production, if the amounts are depletable income to the recipient, and amounts properly allocable to the cost of depreciable property) done by contractors under any form of contract (including a turnkey contract). IDCs include amounts paid for labor, fuel, repairs, hauling, and supplies which are used in the drilling, shooting, and cleaning of wells; in such clearing of ground, draining, road making, surveying, and geological works as are necessary in preparation for the drilling of wells; and in the construction of such derricks, tanks, pipelines, and other physical structures as are necessary for the drilling of wells and the preparation of wells for the production of oil and gas. Generally, IDCs do not include expenses for items which have a salvage value (such as pipes and casings) or items which are part of the acquisition price of an interest in the property.

Under the special rules applicable to IDCs, an operator (i.e., a person who holds a working or operating interest in any tract or parcel of land either as a fee owner or under a lease or any other form of contract granting working or operating rights) who pays or incurs IDCs in the development of an oil or gas property located in the United States may elect either to expense or capitalize those costs. The uniform capitalization rules do not apply to otherwise deductible IDCs.

If a taxpayer elects to expense IDCs, the amount of the IDCs is deductible as an expense in the taxable year the cost is paid or incurred. Generally, IDCs that a taxpayer elects to capitalize may be recovered through depletion or depreciation, as appropriate; or in the case of a nonproductive well ("dry hole"), the operator may elect to deduct the costs. In the case of an integrated oil company (i.e., a company that engages, either directly or through a related enterprise, in substantial retailing or refining activities) that has elected to expense IDCs, 30 percent of the IDCs on productive wells must be capitalized and amortized over a 60-month period.

A taxpayer that has elected to deduct IDCs may, nevertheless, elect to capitalize and amortize certain IDCs over a 60-month period beginning with the month the expenditure was paid or incurred. This rule applies on an expenditure-by-expenditure basis; that is, for any particular taxable year, a taxpayer may deduct some portion of its IDCs and capitalize the rest under this provision. This allows the taxpayer to reduce or eliminate IDC adjustments or preferences under the alternative minimum tax.

The election to deduct IDCs applies only to those IDCs associated with domestic properties. For this purpose, the United States includes certain wells drilled offshore.

Reasons for Change

The President agreed at the G-20 Summit in Pittsburgh to phase out subsidies for fossil fuels so that the United States can transition to a 21st-century energy economy. The expensing of IDCs, like other oil and gas preferences the Administration proposes to repeal, distorts markets by encouraging more investment in the oil and gas industry than would occur under a neutral system. This market distortion is detrimental to long-term energy security and is also inconsistent with the Administration's policy of supporting a clean energy economy, reducing our reliance on oil, and cutting carbon pollution. Moreover, the tax subsidy for oil and gas must ultimately be financed with taxes that result in underinvestment in other, potentially more productive, areas of the economy. Capitalization of IDCs would place the oil and gas industry on a cost recovery system similar to that employed by other industries and reduce economic distortions.

Proposal

The proposal would not allow expensing of intangible drilling costs and 60-month amortization of capitalized intangible drilling costs. Intangible drilling costs would be capitalized as depreciable or depletable property, depending on the nature of the cost incurred, in accordance with the generally applicable rules.

The proposal would be effective for costs paid or incurred after December 31, 2011.

REPEAL DEDUCTION FOR TERTIARY INJECTANTS

Current Law

Taxpayers are allowed to deduct the cost of qualified tertiary injectant expenses for the taxable year. Qualified tertiary injectant expenses are amounts paid or incurred for any tertiary injectants (other than recoverable hydrocarbon injectants) that are used as a part of a tertiary recovery method to increase the recovery of crude oil. The deduction is treated as an amortization deduction in determining the amount subject to recapture upon disposition of the property.

Reasons for Change

The President agreed at the G-20 Summit in Pittsburgh to phase out subsidies for fossil fuels so that the United States can transition to a 21st-century energy economy. The deduction for tertiary injectants, like other oil and gas preferences the Administration proposes to repeal, distorts markets by encouraging more investment in the oil and gas industry than would occur under a neutral system. This market distortion is detrimental to long-term energy security and is also inconsistent with the Administration's policy of supporting a clean energy economy, reducing our reliance on oil, and cutting carbon pollution. Moreover, the tax subsidy for oil and gas must ultimately be financed with taxes that result in underinvestment in other, potentially more productive, areas of the economy. Capitalization of tertiary injectants would place the oil and gas industry on a cost recovery system similar to that employed by other industries and reduce economic distortions.

Proposal

The proposal would not allow the deduction for qualified tertiary injectant expenses for amounts paid or incurred after December 31, 2011.

REPEAL EXCEPTION TO PASSIVE LOSS LIMITATION FOR WORKING INTERESTS IN OIL AND NATURAL GAS PROPERTIES

Current Law

The passive loss rules limit deductions and credits from passive trade or business activities. Deductions attributable to passive activities, to the extent they exceed income from passive activities, generally may not be deducted against other income, such as wages, portfolio income, or business income that is not derived from a passive activity. A similar rule applies to credits. Suspended deductions and credits are carried forward and treated as deductions and credits from passive activities in the next year. The suspended losses and credits from a passive activity are allowed in full when the taxpayer completely disposes of the activity.

Passive activities are defined to include trade or business activities in which the taxpayer does not materially participate. An exception is provided, however, for any working interest in an oil or gas property that the taxpayer holds directly or through an entity that does not limit the liability of the taxpayer with respect to the interest.

Reasons for Change

The President agreed at the G-20 Summit in Pittsburgh to phase out subsidies for fossil fuels so that the United States can transition to a 21st-century energy economy. The special tax treatment of working interests in oil and gas properties, like other oil and gas preferences the Administration proposes to repeal, distorts markets by encouraging more investment in the oil and gas industry than would occur under a neutral system. This market distortion is detrimental to long-term energy security and is also inconsistent with the Administration's policy of supporting a clean energy economy, reducing our reliance on oil, and cutting carbon pollution. Moreover, the working interest exception for oil and gas must ultimately be financed with taxes that result in underinvestment in other, potentially more productive, areas of the economy. Eliminating the working interest exception would subject oil and gas properties to the same limitations as other activities and reduce economic distortions.

Proposal

The proposal would repeal the exception from the passive loss rules for working interests in oil and gas properties for taxable years beginning after December 31, 2011.

REPEAL PERCENTAGE DEPLETION FOR OIL AND NATURAL GAS WELLS

Current Law

The capital costs of oil and gas wells are recovered through the depletion deduction. Under the cost depletion method, the basis recovery for a taxable year is proportional to the exhaustion of the property during the year. This method does not permit cost recovery deductions that exceed basis or that are allowable on an accelerated basis.

A taxpayer may also qualify for percentage depletion with respect to oil and gas properties. The amount of the deduction is a statutory percentage of the gross income from the property. For oil and gas properties, the percentage ranges from 15 to 25 percent and the deduction may not exceed 100 percent of the taxable income from the property. In addition, the percentage depletion deduction for oil and gas properties may not exceed 65 percent of the taxpayer's overall taxable income (determined before the deduction and with certain other adjustments).

Other limitations and special rules apply to the percentage depletion deduction for oil and gas properties. In general, only independent producers and royalty owners (in contrast to integrated oil companies) qualify for the percentage depletion deduction. In addition, oil and gas producers may claim percentage depletion only with respect to up to 1,000 barrels of average daily production of domestic crude oil or an equivalent amount of domestic natural gas (applied on a combined basis in the case of taxpayers that produce both). This quantity limitation is allocated, at the taxpayer's election, between oil production and gas production and then further allocated within each class among the taxpayer's properties. Special rules apply to oil and gas production from marginal wells (generally, wells for which the average daily production is less than 15 barrels of oil or barrel-of-oil equivalents or that produce only heavy oil). Only marginal well production can qualify for percentage depletion at a rate of more than 15 percent. The rate is increased in a taxable year that begins in a calendar year following a calendar year during which the annual average unregulated wellhead price per barrel of domestic crude oil is less than $20. The increase is one percentage point for each whole dollar of difference between the two amounts. In addition, marginal wells are exempt from the 100-percent-of-net-income limitation described above in taxable years beginning during the period 1998-2007 and in taxable years beginning during the period 2009-2011. Unless the taxpayer elects otherwise, marginal well production is given priority over other production in applying the 1,000-barrel limitation on percentage depletion.

A qualifying taxpayer determines the depletion deduction for each oil and gas property under both the percentage depletion method and the cost depletion method and deducts the larger of the two amounts. Because percentage depletion is computed without regard to the taxpayer's basis in the depletable property, a taxpayer may continue to claim percentage depletion after all the expenditures incurred to acquire and develop the property have been recovered.

Reasons for Change

The President agreed at the G-20 Summit in Pittsburgh to phase out subsidies for fossil fuels so that the United States can transition to a 21st-century energy economy. Percentage depletion effectively provides a lower rate of tax with respect to a favored source of income. The lower rate of tax, like other oil and gas preferences the Administration proposes to repeal, distorts markets by encouraging more investment in the oil and gas industry than would occur under a neutral system. This market distortion is detrimental to long-term energy security and is also inconsistent with the Administration's policy of supporting a clean energy economy, reducing our reliance on oil, and cutting carbon pollution. Moreover, the tax subsidy for oil and gas must ultimately be financed with taxes that result in underinvestment in other, potentially more productive, areas of the economy.

Cost depletion computed by reference to the taxpayer's basis in the property is the equivalent of economic depreciation. Limiting oil and gas producers to cost depletion would place them on a cost recovery system similar to that employed by other industries and reduce economic distortions.

Proposal

The proposal would not allow percentage depletion with respect to oil and gas wells. Taxpayers would be permitted to claim cost depletion on their adjusted basis, if any, in oil and gas wells.

The proposal would be effective for taxable years beginning after December 31, 2011.

REPEAL DOMESTIC MANUFACTURING DEDUCTION FOR OIL AND NATURAL GAS COMPANIES

Current Law

A deduction is allowed with respect to income attributable to domestic production activities (the manufacturing deduction). For taxable years beginning after 2009, the manufacturing deduction is generally equal to 9 percent of the lesser of qualified production activities income for the taxable year or taxable income for the taxable year, limited to 50 percent of the W-2 wages of the taxpayer for the taxable year. The deduction for income from oil and gas production activities is computed at a 6 percent rate.

Qualified production activities income is generally calculated as a taxpayer's domestic production gross receipts (i.e., the gross receipts derived from any lease, rental, license, sale, exchange, or other disposition of qualifying production property manufactured, produced, grown, or extracted by the taxpayer in whole or significant part within the United States; any qualified film produced by the taxpayer; or electricity, natural gas, or potable water produced by the taxpayer in the United States) minus the cost of goods sold and other expenses, losses, or deductions attributable to such receipts.

The manufacturing deduction generally is available to all taxpayers that generate qualified production activities income, which under current law includes income from the sale, exchange or disposition of oil, natural gas or primary products thereof produced in the United States.

Reasons for Change

The President agreed at the G-20 Summit in Pittsburgh to phase out subsidies for fossil fuels so that the United States can transition to a 21st-century energy economy. The manufacturing deduction for oil and gas effectively provides a lower rate of tax with respect to a favored source of income. The lower rate of tax, like other oil and gas preferences the Administration proposes to repeal, distorts markets by encouraging more investment in the oil and gas industry than would occur under a neutral system. This market distortion is detrimental to long-term energy security and is also inconsistent with the Administration's policy of supporting a clean energy economy, reducing our reliance on oil, and cutting carbon pollution. Moreover, the tax subsidy for oil and gas must ultimately be financed with taxes that result in underinvestment in other, potentially more productive, areas of the economy.

Proposal

The proposal would retain the overall manufacturing deduction, but exclude from the definition of domestic production gross receipts all gross receipts derived from the sale, exchange or other disposition of oil, natural gas or a primary product thereof for taxable years beginning after December 31, 2011. There is a parallel proposal to repeal the domestic manufacturing deduction for coal and other hard mineral fossil fuels.

INCREASE GEOLOGICAL AND GEOPHYSICAL AMORTIZATION PERIOD FOR INDEPENDENT PRODUCERS TO SEVEN YEARS

Current Law

Geological and geophysical expenditures are costs incurred for the purpose of obtaining and accumulating data that will serve as the basis for the acquisition and retention of mineral properties. The amortization period for geological and geophysical expenditures incurred in connection with oil and gas exploration in the United States is two years for independent producers and seven years for integrated oil and gas producers.

Reasons for Change

The President agreed at the G-20 Summit in Pittsburgh to phase out subsidies for fossil fuels so that the United States can transition to a 21st-century energy economy. The accelerated amortization of geological and geophysical expenditures incurred by independent producers, like other oil and gas preferences the Administration proposes to repeal, distorts markets by encouraging more investment in the oil and gas industry than would occur under a neutral system. This market distortion is detrimental to long-term energy security and is also inconsistent with the Administration's policy of supporting a clean energy economy, reducing our reliance on oil, and cutting carbon pollution. Moreover, the tax subsidy for oil and gas must ultimately be financed with taxes that result in underinvestment in other, potentially more productive, areas of the economy.

Increasing the amortization period for geological and geophysical expenditures incurred by independent oil and gas producers from two years to seven years would provide a more accurate reflection of their income and more consistent tax treatment for all oil and gas producers.

Proposal

The proposal would increase the amortization period from two years to seven years for geological and geophysical expenditures incurred by independent producers in connection with all oil and gas exploration in the United States. Seven-year amortization would apply even if the property is abandoned and any remaining basis of the abandoned property would be recovered over the remainder of the seven-year period.

The proposal would be effective for amounts paid or incurred after December 31, 2011.

Eliminate Coal Preferences

REPEAL EXPENSING OF EXPLORATION AND DEVELOPMENT COSTS

Current Law

In general, costs that benefit future periods must be capitalized and recovered over such periods for income tax purposes, rather than being expensed in the period the costs are incurred. In addition, the uniform capitalization rules require certain direct and indirect costs allocable to property to be included in inventory or capitalized as part of the basis of such property. In general, the uniform capitalization rules apply to real and tangible personal property produced by the taxpayer or acquired for resale.

Special rules apply in the case of mining exploration and development expenditures. A taxpayer may elect to expense the exploration costs incurred for the purpose of ascertaining the existence, location, extent, or quality of an ore or mineral deposit, including a deposit of coal or other hard-mineral fossil fuel. Exploration costs that are expensed are recaptured when the mine reaches the producing stage either by a reduction in depletion deductions or, at the election of the taxpayer, by an inclusion in income in the year in which the mine reaches the producing stage.

After the existence of a commercially marketable deposit has been disclosed, costs incurred for the development of a mine to exploit the deposit are deductible in the year paid or incurred unless the taxpayer elects to deduct the costs on a ratable basis as the minerals or ores produced from the deposit are sold.

In the case of a corporation that elects to deduct exploration costs in the year paid or incurred, 30 percent of the otherwise deductible costs must be capitalized and amortized over a 60-month period. In addition, a taxpayer that has elected to deduct exploration costs may, nevertheless, elect to capitalize and amortize those costs over a 10-year period. This rule applies on an expenditure-by-expenditure basis; that is, for any particular taxable year, a taxpayer may deduct some portion of its exploration costs and capitalize the rest under this provision. This allows the taxpayer to reduce or eliminate adjustments or preferences for exploration costs under the alternative minimum tax. Similar rules limiting corporate deductions and providing for 60-month and 10-year amortization apply with respect to mine development costs.

The election to deduct exploration costs and the rule making development costs deductible in the year paid or incurred apply only with respect to domestic ore and mineral deposits.

Reasons for Change

The President agreed at the G-20 Summit in Pittsburgh to phase out subsidies for fossil fuels so that the United States can transition to a 21st-century energy economy. The expensing of exploration and development costs relating to coal and other hard-mineral fossil fuels, like other fossil-fuel preferences the Administration proposes to repeal, distorts markets by encouraging more investment in fossil-fuel production than would occur under a neutral system. This market distortion is inconsistent with the Administration's policy of supporting a clean energy economy and cutting carbon pollution. Moreover, the tax subsidy for coal and other hard-mineral fossil fuels must ultimately be financed with taxes that result in underinvestment in other, potentially more productive, areas of the economy. Capitalization of exploration and development costs relating to coal and other hard-mineral fossil fuels would place taxpayers in that industry on a cost recovery system similar to that employed by other industries and reduce economic distortions.

Proposal

The proposal would not allow expensing, 60-month amortization, and 10-year amortization of exploration and development costs relating to coal and other hard-mineral fossil fuels. The costs would be capitalized as depreciable or depletable property, depending on the nature of the cost incurred, in accordance with the generally applicable rules. The other hard-mineral fossil fuels for which expensing, 60-month amortization, and 10-year amortization would not be allowed include lignite and oil shale to which a 15-percent depletion rate applies.

The proposal would be effective for costs paid or incurred after December 31, 2011.

REPEAL PERCENTAGE DEPLETION FOR HARD MINERAL FOSSIL FUELS

Current Law

The capital costs of coal mines and other hard-mineral fossil-fuel properties are recovered through the depletion deduction. Under the cost depletion method, the basis recovery for a taxable year is proportional to the exhaustion of the property during the year. This method does not permit cost recovery deductions that exceed basis or that are allowable on an accelerated basis.

A taxpayer may also qualify for percentage depletion with respect to coal and other hard-mineral fossil-fuel properties. The amount of the deduction is a statutory percentage of the gross income from the property. The percentage is 10 percent for coal and lignite and 15 percent for oil shale (other than oil shale to which a 7 ½ percent depletion rate applies because it is used for certain nonfuel purposes). The deduction may not exceed 50 percent of the taxable income from the property (determined before the deductions for depletion and domestic manufacturing).

A qualifying taxpayer determines the depletion deduction for each property under both the percentage depletion method and the cost depletion method and deducts the larger of the two amounts. Because percentage depletion is computed without regard to the taxpayer's basis in the depletable property, a taxpayer may continue to claim percentage depletion after all the expenditures incurred to acquire and develop the property have been recovered.

Reasons for Change

The President agreed at the G-20 Summit in Pittsburgh to phase out subsidies for fossil fuels so that the United States can transition to a 21st-century energy economy. Percentage depletion effectively provides a lower rate of tax with respect to a favored source of income. The lower rate of tax, like other fossil-fuel preferences the Administration proposes to repeal, distorts markets by encouraging more investment in fossil-fuel production than would occur under a neutral system. This market distortion is inconsistent with the Administration's policy of supporting a clean energy economy and cutting carbon pollution. Moreover, the tax subsidy for coal and other hard-mineral fossil fuels must ultimately be financed with taxes that result in underinvestment in other, potentially more productive, areas of the economy.

Cost depletion computed by reference to the taxpayer's basis in the property is the equivalent of economic depreciation. Limiting fossil-fuel producers to cost depletion would place them on a cost recovery system similar to that employed by other industries and reduce economic distortions.

Proposal

The proposal would not allow percentage depletion with respect to coal and other hard-mineral fossil fuels. The other hard-mineral fossil fuels for which no percentage depletion would be allowed include lignite and oil shale to which a 15-percent depletion rate applies. Taxpayers would be permitted to claim cost depletion on their adjusted basis, if any, in coal and other hard-mineral fossil-fuel properties.

The proposal would be effective for taxable years beginning after December 31, 2011.

REPEAL CAPITAL GAINS TREATMENT FOR ROYALTIES

Current Law

Royalties received on the disposition of coal or lignite generally qualify for treatment as long-term capital gain, and the royalty owner does not qualify for percentage depletion with respect to the coal or lignite. This treatment does not apply unless the taxpayer has been the owner of the mineral in place for at least one year before it is mined. The treatment also does not apply to income realized as a co-adventurer, partner, or principal in the mining of the mineral or to certain related-party transactions.

Reasons for Change

The President agreed at the G-20 Summit in Pittsburgh to phase out subsidies for fossil fuels so that the United States can transition to a 21st-century energy economy. The capital gain treatment of coal and lignite royalties, like other fossil-fuel preferences the Administration proposes to repeal, distorts markets by encouraging more investment in fossil-fuel production than would occur under a neutral system. This market distortion is inconsistent with the Administration's policy of supporting a clean energy economy and cutting carbon pollution. Moreover, the tax subsidy for coal and lignite must ultimately be financed with taxes that result in underinvestment in other, potentially more productive, areas of the economy.

Proposal

The proposal would repeal capital gains treatment of coal and lignite royalties and would tax those royalties as ordinary income.

The proposal would be effective for amounts realized in taxable years beginning after December 31, 2011.

REPEAL DOMESTIC MANUFACTURING DEDUCTION FOR COAL AND OTHER HARD MINERAL FOSSIL FUELS

Current Law

A deduction is allowed with respect to income attributable to domestic production activities (the manufacturing deduction). For taxable years beginning after 2009, the manufacturing deduction is generally equal to 9 percent of the lesser of qualified production activities income for the taxable year or taxable income for the taxable year, limited to 50 percent of the W-2 wages of the taxpayer for the taxable year.

Qualified production activities income is generally calculated as a taxpayer's domestic production gross receipts (i.e., the gross receipts derived from any lease, rental, license, sale, exchange, or other disposition of qualifying production property manufactured, produced, grown, or extracted by the taxpayer in whole or significant part within the United States; any qualified film produced by the taxpayer; or electricity, natural gas, or potable water produced by the taxpayer in the United States) minus the cost of goods sold and other expenses, losses, or deductions attributable to such receipts.

The manufacturing deduction generally is available to all taxpayers that generate qualified production activities income, which under current law includes income from the sale, exchange or disposition of coal, other hard-mineral fossil fuels, or primary products thereof produced in the United States.

Reasons for Change

The President agreed at the G-20 Summit in Pittsburgh to phase out subsidies for fossil fuels so that the United States can transition to a 21st-century energy economy. The manufacturing deduction for coal and other hard mineral fossil fuels effectively provides a lower rate of tax with respect to a favored source of income. The lower rate of tax, like other fossil-fuel preferences the Administration proposes to repeal, distorts markets by encouraging more investment in fossil-fuel production than would occur under a neutral system. This market distortion is inconsistent with the Administration's policy of supporting a clean energy economy and cutting carbon pollution. Moreover, the tax subsidy for coal and other hard-mineral fossil fuels must ultimately be financed with taxes that result in underinvestment in other, potentially more productive, areas of the economy.

Proposal

The proposal would retain the overall manufacturing deduction, but exclude from the definition of domestic production gross receipts all gross receipts derived from the sale, exchange or other disposition of coal, other hard-mineral fossil fuels, or a primary product thereof. The hard-mineral fossil fuels to which the exclusion would apply include lignite and oil shale to which a 15-percent depletion rate applies. There is a parallel proposal to repeal the domestic manufacturing deduction for oil and natural gas companies.

The proposal would be effective for taxable years beginning after December 31, 2011.

SIMPLIFY THE TAX CODE

ALLOW VEHICLE SELLER TO CLAIM QUALIFIED PLUG-IN ELECTRIC-DRIVE MOTOR VEHICLE CREDIT

Current Law

A tax credit is provided for plug-in electric drive motor vehicles. A plug-in electric drive motor vehicle is a vehicle that has at least four wheels, is manufactured for use on public roads, is treated as a motor vehicle for purposes of title II of the Clean Air Act (that is, is not a low-speed vehicle), has a gross vehicle weight of less than 14,000 pounds, meets certain emissions standards, draws propulsion energy using a traction battery with at least four kilowatt hours of capacity, is capable of being recharged from an external source, and meets certain other requirements. The credit is $2,500 plus $417 for each kilowatt hour of battery capacity in excess of four kilowatt hours, up to a maximum credit of $7,500. The credit phases out for a manufacturer's vehicles over four calendar quarters beginning with the second calendar quarter following the quarter in which 200,000 of the manufacturer's credit-eligible vehicles have been sold. The credit is generally allowed to the taxpayer that places the vehicle in service (including a person placing the vehicle in service as a lessor). In the case of a vehicle used by a tax-exempt or governmental entity, however, the credit is allowed to the person selling the vehicle to the tax-exempt or governmental entity, but only if the seller clearly discloses the amount of the credit to the purchaser.

Reasons for Change

In 2008, the President set an ambitious goal of putting 1 million advanced technology vehicles on the road by 2015 – which would reduce dependence on foreign oil and lead to a reduction in oil consumption of about 750 million barrels through 2030. To help achieve that goal, the President is proposing increased investment in R&D, a competitive program to encourage communities to invest in electric vehicle infrastructure, and a transformation of the existing tax credit into one that is allowed generally to the seller, which will permit sellers to offer immediate rebates to consumers at the point of sale.

Changing the credit into one that is allowed, in all cases, to the person that sells or finances the sale of the vehicle to the ultimate owner would enable the seller or person financing the sale to offer a point-of-sale rebate to consumers. Disclosure requirements similar to those currently applicable in the case of sales to tax-exempt and governmental entities would ensure that the benefit of the credit is passed on to consumers. Shifting the process of claiming the credit from a large number of individual consumers to a relatively small number of business entities would also simplify tax preparation for individuals and reduce the potential for taxpayer error.

Proposal

The proposal would change the credit from one that is allowed to the person placing the vehicle in service to one that is allowed to the person selling the vehicle to the person placing the vehicle in service (or, at the election of the seller, to the person financing the sale). The credit would be allowed only if the seller (or person financing the sale) clearly discloses the amount of the credit to the purchaser.

The change would be effective for vehicles sold after December 31, 2011.

ELIMINATE MINIMUM REQUIRED DISTRIBUTION (MRD) RULES FOR INDIVIDUAL RETIREMENT ACCOUNT OR ANNUITY (IRA)/PLAN BALANCES OF $50,000 OR LESS

Current Law

The MRD rules generally require that participants in tax-favored retirement plans, including qualified plans under section 401(a), section 401(k) cash or deferred arrangements, section 403(a) annuity plans, section 403(b) programs for public schools and charitable organizations, eligible deferred compensation plans under section 457(b), Simplified Employee Pensions (SEPs), and SIMPLE plans, and owners of IRAs, begin receiving distributions shortly after attaining age 70½. The rules also generally require that these retirement assets be distributed to the plan participant or IRA owner (or their spouses or other beneficiaries), in accordance with regulations, over their life or periods based on their life expectancy (or the joint lives or life expectancies of the participant/owner and beneficiary).[6] Roth IRAs are not subject to the MRD rules during the life of the Roth IRA holder, but the MRD rules do apply to Roth IRAs after the death of the holder.

If a participant or account owner fails to take, in part or in full, the minimum required distribution for a year by the applicable deadline, the amount not withdrawn is subject to a 50-percent excise tax.

Reasons for Change

The MRD rules are designed largely to prevent taxpayers from deferring taxation of amounts that were accorded tax-favored treatment to provide financial security during retirement and instead leaving them to accumulate in tax-exempt arrangements for the benefit of their heirs. Therefore, in the case of taxpayers who have accumulated substantial tax-favored retirement assets, the MRD rules help ensure that tax-favored retirement benefits are in fact used for retirement. Under current law, however, millions of senior citizens with only modest tax-favored retirement benefits to fall back on during retirement also must calculate the amount and timing of their minimum required distributions, even though they are highly unlikely to try to defer withdrawal and taxation of these benefits for estate planning purposes. In addition to simplifying tax compliance for these individuals, the proposal permits them greater flexibility in determining when and how rapidly to draw down their limited retirement savings.

Proposal

The proposal would exempt an individual from the MRD requirements if the aggregate value of the individual's IRA[7] and tax-favored retirement plan accumulations does not exceed $50,000 on a measurement date. However, benefits under qualified defined benefit pension plans that have

---

[6] Participants in tax-favored retirement plans (excluding IRAs) other than owners of at least 5 percent of the business sponsoring the retirement plan may wait to begin distributions until the year of retirement, if that year is later than the year in which the participant reaches age 70 ½ .

[7] While Roth IRAs are exempt from the pre-death MRD rules, amounts held in Roth IRAs would be taken into account in determining whether an individual's aggregate retirement accumulations exceed the $50,000 threshold.

already begun to be paid in life annuity form (including all forms of life annuity, such as joint and survivor, single, life and term certain) would be excluded. The MRD requirements would phase in ratably for individuals with aggregate retirement benefits between $50,000 and $60,000. The initial measurement date for the dollar threshold would be the beginning of the calendar year in which the individual reaches age 70½ or, if earlier, in which the individual dies, with additional measurement dates only at the beginning of the calendar year immediately following any calendar year in which the individual's IRAs or plans receive contributions, rollovers, or transfers of amounts that were not previously taken into account.

The proposal would be effective for taxpayers attaining age 70½ on or after December 31, 2011.

ALLOW ALL INHERITED PLAN AND INDIVIDUAL RETIREMENT ACCOUNT OR ANNUITY (IRA) BALANCES TO BE ROLLED OVER WITHIN 60 DAYS

Current Law

Generally, assets can be moved from a tax-favored employer retirement plan or from an IRA into an IRA or into an eligible retirement plan without adverse tax consequences. This movement of assets can generally be accomplished through a direct rollover of a distribution, a 60-day rollover, or a direct trustee-to-trustee transfer that is not a distribution. However, not all of these methods are available with respect to assets of a plan or IRA account inherited by a non-spouse beneficiary.

In particular, when a participant in a tax-favored employer retirement plan dies before all assets in the plan have been distributed, a beneficiary who is a surviving spouse may roll over the assets, by direct rollover or 60-day rollover, into an IRA that is treated either as a spousal inherited IRA or as the surviving spouse's own IRA. A beneficiary who is not a surviving spouse, on the other hand, may roll over the assets into an IRA that is a non-spousal inherited IRA only by means of a direct rollover; a 60-day rollover is not available to a surviving non-spouse beneficiary.

Similarly, when the owner of an IRA dies before all assets in the IRA have been distributed, a surviving spouse beneficiary may elect to treat the assets as his or her own IRA or as a spousal inherited IRA. In addition, a surviving spouse beneficiary may roll over the assets into an IRA that is treated either as the surviving spouse's own IRA or as a spousal inherited IRA. A surviving non-spouse beneficiary, on the other hand, may treat the assets as a non-spousal inherited IRA, and may move the assets to another non-spousal inherited IRA only by means of a direct trustee-to-trustee transfer; rollovers from the deceased owner's IRA to another IRA are not available for a surviving non-spouse beneficiary.

Reasons for Change

The rules that a surviving non-spouse beneficiary under a tax-favored employer retirement plan may roll over assets to an IRA only by means of a direct rollover and that a surviving non-spouse beneficiary under an IRA may move assets to a non-spousal inherited IRA only by means of a direct trustee-to-trustee transfer create traps for the unwary. These differences in rollover eligibility between surviving non-spouse beneficiaries and surviving spouse beneficiaries (and living participants) serve little purpose and generate confusion among plan and IRA administrators and beneficiaries. For example, IRA administrators often treat all transfers (whether or not an IRA account is a non-spousal inherited IRA) as rollovers, thereby causing confusion for individuals and the Internal Revenue Service. Similarly non-spouse beneficiaries may attempt to move assets to an inherited IRA by means of a 60-day rollover.

Proposal

The proposal would expand the options that are available to a surviving non-spouse beneficiary under a tax-favored employer retirement plan or IRA for moving inherited plan or IRA assets to a non-spousal inherited IRA by allowing 60-day rollovers of such assets.

The proposal would be effective for distributions after December 31, 2011.

CLARIFY EXCEPTION TO RECAPTURE OF UNRECOGNIZED GAIN ON SALE OF STOCK TO AN EMPLOYEE STOCK OWNERSHIP PLAN (ESOP)

Current Law

Section 1042 allows a taxpayer to elect to defer the recognition of long-term capital gain on the sale of employer securities to an ESOP under certain circumstances and subject to certain conditions, including purchase of qualified replacement property within a specified period. The deferred gain is subject to recapture on disposition of the qualified replacement property unless an exception applies. One of the exceptions is for a disposition by gift.

Reasons for Change

Section 1041 generally provides that no gain or loss is recognized on a transfer of property between spouses, including former spouses if incident to divorce, treating such a transfer instead as a gift received by the transferee. However, section 1041 does not expressly address the treatment of the transferor, and section 1042 provides no express exception to the recapture rules for a nontaxable transfer of qualified replacement property to a spouse, including pursuant to a divorce, under section 1041. This has given rise to questions as to whether a transfer incident to a divorce is a disposition that triggers recapture under 1042.

Proposal

The proposal would amend the recapture rules of section 1042 to provide an exception for transfers under section 1041.

The proposal would be effective with respect to transfers made under section 1041 after December 31, 2011. No inference as to prior law is intended.

REPEAL NON-QUALIFIED PREFERRED STOCK (NQPS) DESIGNATION

Current Law

In 1997 Congress added a provision to section 351 that treats NQPS as taxable "boot" for certain purposes. In addition to its treatment as boot in corporate organizations, NQPS is also treated as boot in certain shareholder exchanges pursuant to a plan of corporate reorganization. NQPS is stock that (i) is limited and preferred as to dividends and does not participate in corporate growth to any significant extent; and (ii) has a dividend rate that varies with reference to an index, or, in certain circumstances, a put right, a call right, or a mandatory redemption feature. The addition of this provision reflected the belief that the receipt of certain types of preferred stock more appropriately represented taxable consideration because the investor/transferor obtained a more secure form of investment.

Reasons for Change

NQPS is treated like debt for certain limited purposes but is otherwise generally treated as stock. This hybrid nature of NQPS has transformed it into a staple of affirmative corporate tax planning: its issuance often occurs in loss-recognition planning, where NQPS is treated as debt-like boot, or to avoid the application of a provision that treats a related-party stock sale as a dividend. Thus, for the unwary, the designation and treatment of NQPS represents a proverbial trap that adds additional complexity to the tax code, while for the well-advised, the issuance of NQPS often arises in transactions that are inconsistent with the original purpose of the 1997 provision.

Proposal

The proposal would repeal the NQPS provision and other cross-referencing provisions of the Code that treat NQPS as boot.

The proposal would be effective for stock issued after December 31, 2011.

REVISE AND SIMPLIFY THE "FRACTIONS RULE"

Current Law

Section 514(a) generally provides that a tax-exempt organization will recognize unrelated business taxable income (UBTI) with respect to debt-financed property. In order to allow certain organizations to participate in ordinary real estate transactions, section 514(c)(9) excepts indebtedness incurred by a qualified organization in acquiring or improving any real property. Qualified organizations include certain educational organizations, pension funds, and title trusts. If a qualified organization invests in real property through a partnership that has incurred indebtedness, in order to qualify under section 514(c)(9), the partnership must consist entirely of qualified funds, have entirely pro rata allocations, or have allocations that satisfy the fractions rule described in section 514(c)(9)(E). The fractions rule generally provides that the allocation of items to any partner which is a qualified organization cannot result in such partner having a share of the overall partnership income for any taxable year greater than such partner's share of the overall partnership loss for the taxable year for which such partner's loss share will be the smallest, and each allocation with respect to the partnership must have substantial economic effect within the meaning of section 704(b)(2). Allocations under section 704(c) of built-in gain and built-in loss are not taken into account in applying the fractions rule, nor are certain chargebacks, preferred returns, and guaranteed payments.

Under section 704(b), a partner's distributive share of income, gain, loss, deduction, or credit (or item thereof) is determined in accordance with the partner's interest in the partnership if: (1) the partnership agreement does not specify the partner's distributive share of the item, or (2) the allocation to a partner under the agreement does not have substantial economic effect. The regulations under section 704(b) further define the substantial economic effect test. Under those regulations, a partnership's allocations will have substantial economic effect if the partnership maintains capital accounts for its partners in compliance with numerous technical rules, the partnership liquidates according to those capital account balances, and the partnership's allocations do not violate an anti-abuse rule commonly referred to as the "substantiality test." Special rules apply to losses financed by nonrecourse debt.

Reasons for Change

The fractions rule was enacted to prevent tax abuses that could arise in situations where a partnership allocates its income to exempt organizations and its losses to taxable persons. The fractions rule has been heavily criticized for its complexity and its unnecessary hindrance to qualified organizations entering into ordinary, commercially reasonable business transactions.

Since the fractions rule was first adopted in 1984, a number of additional limitations have been placed on the ability of taxable investors in real estate partnerships to use the tax benefits generated by those partnerships. These include: (1) the expansion and refinement of the substantial economic effect rules; (2) the lengthening of the depreciation period for commercial real estate; (3) the enactment of the passive activity loss and at risk rules; and (4) the strengthening of the alternative minimum tax. These developments alleviate the need for a strict, formulaic fractions rule.

Proposal

The proposal would replace the fractions rule with a rule that requires each partnership allocation to have substantial economic effect (as required by current law) and no allocation to have a principal purpose of tax avoidance. Regulatory authority would be granted to eliminate the "cliff effect" of a technical violation of the rule.

The proposal would be effective as of the date of enactment.

REPEAL PREFERENTIAL DIVIDEND RULE FOR PUBLICLY TRADED REAL ESTATE INVESTMENT TRUSTS (REITS)

Current Law

REITs are allowed a deduction for dividends paid to their shareholders. In order to qualify for the deduction, a dividend must not be a "preferential dividend."[8] For this purpose, a dividend is preferential unless it is distributed pro rata to shareholders, with no preference to any share of stock compared with other shares of the same class, and with no preference to one class as compared with another except to the extent the class is entitled to a preference. Until last year, a similar rule had applied to all regulated investment companies (RICs). Section 307 of the Regulated Investment Company Modernization Act of 2010 (Pub. L. No. 111–325) repealed application of that rule for publicly offered RICs.

Reasons for Change

The original purpose of the preferential dividend rule in 1936 was to prevent tax avoidance by closely held personal holding companies. The inflexibility of the rule can produce harsh results for inadvertent deviations in the timing or amount of distributions to some shareholders. Because an attempt to compensate for a preference in one distribution produces a preference in a second offsetting distribution, it is almost impossible to undo the impact of a prior error.

As applied to publicly traded REITs, the rule has ceased to serve a necessary function either in preventing tax avoidance or in ensuring fairness among shareholders. Today, for these shareholders, corporate and securities laws bar preferences and ensure fair treatment.

Proposal

The proposal would repeal the preferential dividend rule for publicly traded REITs. The Treasury Department would also be given explicit authority to provide for cures of inadvertent violations of the preferential dividend rule where it continues to apply and, where appropriate, to require consistent treatment of shareholders.

The proposal would apply to distributions that are made (without regard to section 858) in taxable years beginning after the date of enactment.

---

[8] Section 562(c).

REFORM EXCISE TAX BASED ON INVESTMENT INCOME OF PRIVATE FOUNDATIONS

Current Law

Private foundations that are exempt from federal income tax generally are subject to a two-percent excise tax on their net investment income. The excise tax rate is reduced to one percent in any year in which the foundation's distributions for charitable purposes exceed the average level of the foundation's charitable distributions over the five preceding taxable years (with certain adjustments). Private foundations that are not exempt from federal income tax, including certain charitable trusts, must pay an excise tax equal to the excess (if any) of the sum of the excise tax on net investment income and the amount of the unrelated business income tax that would have been imposed if the foundation were tax exempt, over the income tax imposed on the foundation. Under current law, private nonoperating foundations generally are required to make annual distributions for charitable purposes equal to five percent of the fair market value of the foundation's noncharitable use assets (with certain adjustments). The amount that a foundation is required to distribute annually for charitable purposes is reduced by the amount of the excise tax paid by the foundation.

Reasons for Change

The current "two-tier" structure of the excise tax on private foundation net investment income may discourage foundations from significantly increasing their charitable distributions in any particular year. An increase in a private foundation's distributions in one year will increase the foundation's five-year average percentage payout, making it more difficult for the foundation to qualify for the reduced one-percent excise tax rate in subsequent years. Because amounts paid by foundations in excise tax generally reduce the funds available for distribution to charitable beneficiaries, eliminating the "two-tier" structure of this excise tax would ensure that a private foundation's grantees do not suffer adverse consequences if the foundation increases its grantmaking in a particular year to respond to charitable needs (for example, disaster relief). Such a change would also simplify both the calculation of the excise tax and charitable distribution planning for private foundations.

Proposal

This proposal would replace the two rates of tax on private foundations that are exempt from federal income tax with a single tax rate of 1.35 percent. The tax on private foundations not exempt from federal income tax would be equal to the excess (if any) of the sum of the 1.35-percent excise tax on net investment income and the amount of the unrelated business income tax that would have been imposed if the foundation were tax exempt, over the income tax imposed on the foundation. The special reduced excise tax rate available to tax-exempt private foundations that maintain their historic level of charitable distributions would be repealed.

The proposal would be effective for taxable years beginning after the date of enactment.

Simplify Tax-Exempt Bonds

SIMPLIFY ARBITRAGE INVESTMENT RESTRICTIONS

Current Law

Section 103 provides generally that interest on debt obligations issued by State and local governments for governmental purposes is excludable from gross income. Section 148 imposes two types of complex arbitrage investment restrictions on investments of tax-exempt bond proceeds pending use for governmental purposes. These restrictions generally limit investment returns that exceed the yield or effective interest rate on the tax-exempt bonds. One type of restriction, called "yield restriction," limits investment returns in the first instance, and a second type, called "rebate," requires issuers to repay arbitrage investment earnings to the Federal Government at prescribed intervals. These restrictions developed in different ways over a long period of time, beginning with yield restriction in 1969 and continuing with the extension of the rebate requirement to all tax-exempt bonds in 1986. Various exceptions apply in different ways to these two types of arbitrage restrictions, including exceptions for prompt expenditures of bond proceeds, reasonable debt service reserve funds, small issuers, and other situations.

With respect to spending exceptions, a two-year construction spending exception to arbitrage rebate under section 148(f)(4)(C) applies to certain categories of tax-exempt bonds (including bonds for governmental entities and nonprofit entities, but excluding most private activity bonds). This two-year construction spending exception has semiannual spending targets, bifurcation rules to isolate construction expenditures, and elective penalties in lieu of rebate for failures to meet spending targets. Separately, a longstanding regulatory three-year spending exception to yield restriction is available for all tax-exempt bonds used for capital projects.

A small issuer exception to arbitrage rebate under section 148(f)(4)(D) applies to certain governmental small issuers with general taxing powers if they issue no more than $5 million in tax-exempt bonds in a particular year. The small issuer exception has been in effect since 1986 without change, except for an increase to $15 million for certain public school expenditures.

Reasons for Change

The arbitrage investment restrictions create unnecessary complexity and compliance burdens for State and local governments in several respects. In general, the two types of arbitrage restrictions (yield restriction and rebate) are duplicative and overlapping and they have the same tax policy objective to limit arbitrage profit incentives for excess issuance of tax-exempt bonds. While Treasury Regulations have integrated these restrictions partially, further statutory integration of the arbitrage restrictions could provide a simpler and more unified framework.

Moreover, the two-year construction spending exception to arbitrage rebate is extremely complex. This exception has restricted eligibility rules, unduly-short spending targets, and complex penalty elections that are rarely used. A streamlined spending exception could provide meaningful simplification and reduce compliance burdens. Limited arbitrage potential exists if issuers spend proceeds fairly promptly. By comparison, a recent uniform provision for qualified

93

tax credit bonds under section 54A has a simplified three-year spending exception to arbitrage restrictions, along with a requirement to redeem bonds upon a failure to meet the spending rules.

An increase in the small issuer exception to arbitrage rebate would reduce compliance burdens for a large number of State and local governmental issuers while affecting a disproportionately smaller amount of tax-exempt bond dollar volume. For example, in 2008, issuers under a similar $10 million small issuer exception for bank-qualified tax-exempt bonds under section 265 issued about 39 percent of the total number of tax-exempt bond issues (4,195 out of 10,830 total bond issues), but only 3.9 percent of total dollar volume ($15.3 billion out of $389.6 billion).

Proposal

Unify Yield Restriction and Rebate Further. The proposal would unify yield restriction and rebate further. The proposal would rely on arbitrage rebate as the principal type of arbitrage restriction on tax-exempt bonds. The proposal generally would repeal yield restriction, subject to limited exceptions under which yield restriction would continue to apply to investments of refunding escrows in advance refunding issues under section 149(d) and to other situations identified in regulations.

Broader Streamlined Three-year Spending Exception. The proposal would provide a broader streamlined three-year spending exception to arbitrage rebate for tax-exempt bonds which meet the following requirements:

(1) Eligible Tax-exempt Bonds. Eligible tax-exempt bonds would include all governmental bonds and private activity bonds, excluding only bonds used for advance refundings under section 149(d) or restricted working capital expenditures (as defined in regulations).
(2) Long-term Fixed Rate Bonds. The tax-exempt bonds would be required to have a fixed yield and a minimum weighted average maturity of at least five years.
(3) Spending Period. The issuer would be required to spend 95 percent of the bond within three years after the issue date.
(This 5 percent de minimis provision broadens the availability exception to cover many circumstances in which minor amounts of bond proceed remain unspent for bona fide reasons.)
(4) Due Diligence. The issuer would be required to proceed with due diligence to spend the bond proceeds.

Upon a failure to meet the spending requirements for this exception, the tax-exempt bond issue would revert to become subject to the arbitrage rebate requirement.

Increase Small Issuer Exception. The proposal would increase the small issuer exception to the arbitrage rebate requirement for tax-exempt bonds from $5 million to $10 million and index the size limit for inflation. The proposal also would remove the general taxing power constraint on small issuer eligibility.

The proposal would be effective for bonds issued after the date of enactment.

SIMPLIFY SINGLE-FAMILY HOUSING MORTGAGE BOND TARGETING REQUIREMENTS

Current Law

Section 143 allows use of tax-exempt qualified mortgage bonds to finance mortgage loans for owner-occupied single-family housing residences, subject to a number of targeting requirements, including, among others: a mortgagor income limitation (generally not more than 115 percent of applicable median family income, increased to 140 percent of such income for certain targeted areas, and also increased for certain high-cost areas); a purchase price limitation (generally not more than 90 percent of average area purchase prices, increased to 110 percent in targeted areas); refinancing limitation (generally only new mortgages for first-time homebuyers are eligible); and a targeted area availability requirement. In addition, the general restrictions on tax-exempt private activity bonds apply to these qualified mortgage bonds, including, among other restrictions, the State private activity bond volume cap under section 146.

Reasons for Change

The targeting requirements for qualified mortgage bonds are complex and excessive. The mortgagor income limit generally serves as an appropriate limit to target this lower cost borrowing subsidy to a needy class of low and moderate income beneficiaries. The mortgagor income limit typically is a more constraining factor than the purchase price limit. The restriction against refinancing limits the availability of this lower cost borrowing subsidy as a tool to address needs for affordable mortgage loan refinancing within a needy class of existing low and moderate income homeowners.

Proposal

The proposal would repeal the purchase price limitation under section 143(e) and the refinancing limitation under section 143(d) on tax-exempt qualified mortgage bonds.

This proposal would be effective for bonds issued after the date of enactment.

STREAMLINE PRIVATE BUSINESS LIMITS ON GOVERNMENTAL BONDS

Current Law

Section 141 treats tax-exempt bonds issued by State and local governments as governmental bonds if the issuer limits private business use and other private involvement sufficiently to avoid treatment as "private activity bonds." Bonds generally are classified as private activity bonds under a two-part test if more than 10 percent of the bond proceeds are both (i) used for private business use, and (ii) payable or secured from property or payments derived from private business use.

Subsidiary restrictions further reduce the permitted thresholds of private involvement for governmental bonds in several ways. Section 141(b)(3) imposes a 5 percent unrelated or disproportionate private business use limit. Section 141(b)(4) imposes a $15 million cap on private business involvement for governmental output facilities (such as electric, gas, or other output generation, transmission, and distribution facilities, but excluding water facilities). Section 141(c) imposes a private loan limit equal to the lesser of 5 percent or $5 million of bond proceeds. Section 141(b)(5) requires a volume cap allocation for private business involvement that exceeds $15 million in larger transactions which otherwise comply with the general 10 percent private business limits.

Reasons for Change

The 10 percent private business limit generally represents a sufficient and workable threshold for governmental bond status. The volume cap requirement for private business involvement in excess of $15 million serves a control on private business involvement in larger transactions.

The particular subsidiary restriction which imposes a 5 percent limit on unrelated or disproportionate private business use introduces undue complexity, a narrow disqualification trigger, and attendant compliance burdens for State and local governments. The 5 percent unrelated or disproportionate private business use test requires difficult factual determinations regarding the relationship of private business use to governmental use in financed projects. This test is difficult to apply, particularly in governmental bond issues that finance multiple projects.

Proposal

The proposal would repeal the 5 percent unrelated or disproportionate private business use test under section 141(b)(3) to simplify the private business limits on tax-exempt governmental bonds.

This proposal would be effective for bonds issued after the date of enactment.

REDUCE THE TAX GAP AND MAKE REFORMS

Expand Information Reporting

REPEAL AND MODIFY INFORMATION REPORTING ON PAYMENTS TO CORPORATIONS AND PAYMENTS FOR PROPERTY

Current Law

Generally, a taxpayer making payments to a recipient aggregating to $600 or more for services or determinable gains in the course of a trade or business in a calendar year is required to send an information return to the Internal Revenue Service (IRS) setting forth the amount, as well as name and address of the recipient of the payment (generally on Form 1099). Under a longstanding regulatory regime, there were certain exceptions for payments to corporations, as well as tax-exempt and government entities. Also, this information reporting requirement did not apply to payments for property.

Effective for payments made after December 31, 2011, the Affordable Care Act expanded the information reporting requirement to include payments to a corporation (except a tax-exempt corporation) and payments for property.

Reasons for Change

Generally, compliance increases significantly for payments that a third party reports to the IRS. In the case of payments to tax-exempt or government entities that are generally not subject to income tax, information returns may not be necessary. On the other hand, during the decades in which the regulatory exception for payments to corporations has become established, the number and complexity of corporate taxpayers have increased. Moreover, the longstanding regulatory exception from information reporting for payments to corporations has created compliance issues. In addition, the expanded information reporting requirements imposed by the Affordable Care Act will put an undue burden on small businesses.

Proposal

The proposal would repeal the additional information reporting requirements imposed by the Affordable Care Act. Further, the proposal would require businesses to file an information return for payments for services or for determinable gains aggregating to $600 or more in a calendar year to a corporation (except a tax-exempt corporation). Regulatory authority would be provided to make appropriate exceptions where reporting would be especially burdensome. Information returns would not be required for payments for property.

This proposal would be effective for payments made after December 31, 2011.

REQUIRE INFORMATION REPORTING FOR PRIVATE SEPARATE ACCOUNTS OF LIFE INSURANCE COMPANIES

Current Law

Earnings from direct investment in securities generally result in taxable income to the holder. In contrast, investments in comparable assets through a separate account of a life insurance company generally give rise to tax-free or tax-deferred income. This favorable tax treatment for investing through a life insurance company is not available if the policyholder has so much control over the investments in the separate account that the policyholder, rather than the insurance company, is treated as the owner of those investments.

Reasons for Change

In some cases, private separate accounts are being used to avoid tax that would be due if the assets were held directly. Better reporting of investments in private separate accounts will help the Internal Revenue Service (IRS) to ensure that income is properly reported. Moreover, such reporting will enable the IRS to identify more easily which variable insurance contracts qualify as insurance contracts under current law and which contracts should be disregarded under the investor control doctrine.

Proposal

The proposal would require life insurance companies to report to the IRS, for each contract whose cash value is partially or wholly invested in a private separate account for any portion of the taxable year and represents at least 10 percent of the value of the account, the policyholder's taxpayer identification number, the policy number, the amount of accumulated untaxed income, the total contract account value, and the portion of that value that was invested in one or more private separate accounts. For this purpose, a private separate account would be defined as any account with respect to which a related group of persons owns policies whose cash values, in the aggregate, represent at least 10 percent of the value of the separate account. Whether a related group of persons owns policies whose cash values represent at least 10 percent of the value of the account would be determined quarterly, based on information reasonably within the issuer's possession.

The proposal would be effective for taxable years beginning after December 31, 2011.

REQUIRE A CERTIFIED TAXPAYER IDENTIFICATION NUMBER (TIN) FROM CONTRACTORS AND ALLOW CERTAIN WITHHOLDING

Current Law

In the course of a trade or business, service recipients ("businesses") making payments aggregating to $600 or more in a calendar year to any non-employee service provider ("contractor") that is not a corporation are required to send an information return to the Internal Revenue Service (IRS) setting forth the amount, as well as name, address, and TIN of the contractor. The information returns, required annually after the end of the year, are made on Form 1099-MISC based on identifying information furnished by the contractor but not verified by the IRS. Copies are provided both to the contractor and to the IRS. Withholding is not required or permitted for payments to contractors. Since contractors are not subject to withholding, they may be required to make quarterly payments of estimated income taxes and self-employment (SECA) taxes near the end of each calendar quarter. The contractor is required to pay any balance due when the annual income tax return is subsequently filed.

Reasons for Change

Without accurate taxpayer identifying information, information reporting requirements impose avoidable burdens on businesses and the IRS, and cannot reach their potential to improve compliance.

Estimated tax filing is relatively burdensome, especially for less sophisticated and lower-income taxpayers. Moreover, by the time estimated tax payments (or final tax payments) are due, some contractors will not have put aside the necessary funds. Given that the SECA tax rate is 15.3 percent (up to certain income limits), the required estimated tax payments can be more than 25 percent of a contractor's gross receipts, even for a contractor with modest income.

An optional withholding method for contractors would reduce the burdens of having to make quarterly payments, would help contractors automatically set aside funds for tax payments, and would help increase compliance.

Proposal

The proposal would require a contractor receiving payments of $600 or more in a calendar year from a particular business to furnish to the business (on Form W-9) the contractor's certified TIN. A business would be required to verify the contractor's TIN with the IRS, which would be authorized to disclose, solely for this purpose, whether the certified TIN-name combination matches IRS records. If a contractor failed to furnish an accurate certified TIN, the business would be required to withhold a flat-rate percentage of gross payments. Contractors receiving payments of $600 or more in a calendar year from a particular business could require the business to withhold a flat-rate percentage of their gross payments, with the flat-rate percentage of 15, 25, 30, or 35 percent being selected by the contractor.

The proposal would be effective for payments made to contractors after December 31, 2011.

Improve Compliance by Businesses

REQUIRE GREATER ELECTRONIC FILING OF RETURNS

Current Law

Corporations with assets of $10 million or more filing Form 1120 are required to file Schedule M-3 (Net Income (Loss) Reconciliation for Corporations with Total Assets of $10 Million or More). This Schedule M-3 filing requirement also applies to S corporations, life insurance corporations, property and casualty insurance corporations, and cooperative associations filing various versions of Form 1120 and having $10 million or more in assets. Schedule M-3 is also required for partnerships with assets of $10 million or more and certain other partnerships.

Corporations and tax-exempt organizations that have assets of $10 million or more and file at least 250 returns during a calendar year, including income tax, information, excise tax, and employment tax returns, are required to file electronically their Form 1120/1120S income tax returns and Form 990 information returns. In addition, private foundations and charitable trusts that file at least 250 returns during a calendar year are required to file electronically their Form 990-PF information returns, regardless of their asset size. Taxpayers can request waivers of the electronic filing requirement if they cannot meet that requirement due to technological constraints, or if compliance with the requirement would result in undue financial burden on the taxpayer. Although electronic filing is required of certain corporations and other taxpayers, others may convert voluntarily to electronic filing.

Generally, regulations may require electronic filing by taxpayers (other than individuals, estates and trusts) that file at least 250 returns annually. Before requiring electronic filing, the Internal Revenue Service (IRS) and Treasury Department must take into account the ability of taxpayers to comply at a reasonable cost.

Reasons for Change

Generally, compliance increases when taxpayers are required to provide better information to the IRS in usable form. Large organizations with assets of $10 million or more generally maintain financial records in electronic form, and generally either hire tax professionals who use tax preparation software or use tax preparation software themselves although they may not currently file electronically.

Electronic filing supports the broader goals of improving IRS service to taxpayers, enhancing compliance, and modernizing tax administration. Overall, increased electronic filing of returns may improve customer satisfaction and confidence in the filing process, and it may be more cost effective for affected entities. Expanding electronic filing to certain additional large entities will help provide tax return information in a more uniform electronic form. This will enhance the ability of the IRS to more productively focus its audit activities. This can reduce burdens on businesses where the need for an audit can be avoided.

In the case of a large business, adopting the same standard for electronic filing as for filing Schedule M-3 provides simplification benefits.

Proposal

The proposal would require to all those corporations and partnerships that must file Schedule M-3 to file their tax returns electronically. In the case of certain other large taxpayers not required to file Schedule M-3 (such as exempt organizations), the regulatory authority to require electronic filing would be expanded to allow reduction of the current threshold of filing 250 or more returns during a calendar year. Additionally, the regulatory authority would be expanded to allow reduction of the 250-return threshold in the case of information returns such as those required by Subpart B, Part III, Subchapter A, Chapter 61, Subtitle F, of the Internal Revenue Code (generally Forms 1099, 1098, 1096, and 5498). Nevertheless, any new regulations would balance the benefits of electronic filing against any burden that might be imposed on taxpayers, and implementation would take place incrementally to afford adequate time for transition to electronic filing. Taxpayers would be able to request waivers of this requirement if they cannot meet the requirement due to technological constraints, if compliance with the requirement would result in undue financial burden, or if other criteria specified in regulations are met.

The proposal would be effective for taxable years ending after December 31, 2011.

AUTHORIZE THE DEPARTMENT OF THE TREASURY TO REQUIRE ADDITIONAL INFORMATION TO BE INCLUDED IN ELECTRONICALLY FILED FORM 5500 ANNUAL REPORTS

Current Law

Code section 6058 requires the sponsor of a funded plan of deferred compensation (or the administrator of the plan) to file an annual return containing certain information in accordance with regulations prescribed by the Secretary of the Treasury. Section 6059 requires that a pension plan subject to the minimum funding requirements of section 412 file an actuarial report prepared by an enrolled actuary. Similarly, Title I of the Employee Retirement Income Security Act of 1974 (ERISA) requires that certain pension and welfare benefit plans file an annual report disclosing certain information to the Department of Labor (DOL). These Code and ERISA filing requirements have been consolidated into a single series of forms (Form 5500 and attachments) that is filed with the DOL and then shared with the Internal Revenue Service (IRS). This filing serves as the primary tool for gathering information and for appropriate targeting of enforcement activity regarding such plans. It also serves to satisfy certain requirements for filing with the Pension Benefit Guaranty Corporation.

Reasons for Change

The Department of Labor has the authority to require electronic filing of information relevant to Title I of ERISA and has exercised its authority to require that Form 5500 and its attachments be filed electronically. However, under section 6011(e), the Treasury and IRS lack general statutory authority to require electronic filing of returns unless the person subject to the filing requirement must file at least 250 returns during the year. As a result, information relevant only to tax code requirements (such as data on coverage needed to test compliance with nondiscrimination rules) and not to DOL's ERISA Title I jurisdiction cannot be requested on the electronically-filed joint Form 5500 and currently is not collected. Collecting it would require a separate "IRS only" form that could be filed on paper, a process that would be neither simple nor efficient for taxpayers or for the IRS and DOL.

Proposal

The proposal would provide the IRS the authority to require in the electronically filed annual reports the inclusion of information that is relevant only to employee benefit plan tax requirements, giving the IRS authority with respect to such tax information comparable to that DOL already has with respect to information relevant to ERISA Title I.

The proposal would be effective for plan years beginning after December 31, 2011.

IMPLEMENT STANDARDS CLARIFYING WHEN EMPLOYEE LEASING COMPANIES CAN BE HELD LIABLE FOR THEIR CLIENTS' FEDERAL EMPLOYMENT TAXES

Current Law

Employers are required to withhold and pay Federal Insurance Contribution Act (FICA) taxes and to withhold and remit income taxes, and are required to pay Federal Unemployment Tax Act (FUTA) taxes (collectively "Federal employment taxes") with respect to wages paid to their employees. Liability for Federal employment taxes generally lies with the taxpayer that is determined to be the employer under a multi-factor common law test or under specific statutory provisions. For example, a third party that is not the common law employer can be a statutory employer if the third party has control over the payment of wages. In addition, certain designated agents are jointly and severally liable with their principals for employment taxes with respect to wages paid to the principals' employees. These designated agents prepare and file employment tax returns using their own name and employer identification number. In contrast, reporting agents (often referred to as payroll service providers) are generally not liable for the employment taxes reported on their clients' returns. Reporting agents prepare and file employment tax returns for their clients using the client's name and employer identification number.

Employee leasing is the practice of contracting with an outside business to handle certain administrative, personnel, and payroll matters for a taxpayer's employees. Employee leasing companies (often referred to as professional employer organizations) typically prepare and file employment tax returns for their clients using the leasing company's name and employer identification number, often taking the position that the leasing company is the statutory or common law employer of their clients' workers.

Reasons for Change

Under present law, there is often uncertainty as to whether the employee leasing company or its client is liable for unpaid Federal employment taxes arising with respect to wages paid to the client's workers. Thus, when an employee leasing company files employment tax returns using its own name and employer identification number, but fails to pay some or all of the taxes due, or when no returns are filed with respect to wages paid by a taxpayer that uses an employee leasing company, there can be uncertainty as to how the Federal employment taxes are assessed and collected.

Providing standards for when an employee leasing company and its clients will be held liable for Federal employment taxes will facilitate the assessment, payment and collection of those taxes and will preclude taxpayers who have control over withholding and payment of those taxes from denying liability when the taxes are not paid.

Proposal

The proposal would set forth standards for holding employee leasing companies jointly and severally liable with their clients for Federal employment taxes. The proposal would also provide standards for holding employee leasing companies solely liable for such taxes if they meet specified requirements.

The provision would be effective for employment tax returns required to be filed with respect to wages paid after December 31, 2011.

INCREASE CERTAINTY WITH RESPECT TO WORKER CLASSIFICATION

Current Law

For both tax and nontax purposes, workers must be classified into one of two mutually exclusive categories: employees or self-employed (sometimes referred to as independent contractors).

Worker classification generally is based on a common-law test for determining whether an employment relationship exists. The main determinant is whether the service recipient (employer) has the right to control not only the result of the worker's services but also the means by which the worker accomplishes that result. For classification purposes, it does not matter whether the service recipient exercises that control, only that he or she has the right to exercise it. Even though it is generally recognized that more highly skilled workers may not require much guidance or direction from the service recipient, the underlying concept of the right to control is the same for them. In addition, only individuals can be employees. In determining worker status, the Internal Revenue Service (IRS) looks to three categories of evidence that may be relevant in determining whether the requisite control exists under the common-law test: behavioral control, financial control, and the relationship of the parties.

For employees, employers are required to withhold income and Federal Insurance Contribution Act (FICA) taxes and to pay the employer's share of FICA taxes. Employers are also required to pay Federal Unemployment Tax Act (FUTA) taxes and generally state unemployment compensation taxes. Liability for Federal employment taxes and the obligation to report the wages generally lie with the employer.

For workers who are classified as independent contractors, service recipients engaged in a trade or business and that make payments totaling $600 or more in a calendar year to an independent contractor that is not a corporation are required to send an information return to the IRS and to the independent contractor stating the total payments made during the year. The service recipient generally does not need to withhold taxes from the payments reported unless the independent contractor has not provided its taxpayer identification number to the service recipient. Independent contractors pay Self-Employment Contributions Act (SECA) tax on their net earnings from self-employment (which generally is equivalent to both the employer and employee shares of FICA tax). Independent contractors generally are required to pay their income tax, including SECA liabilities, by making quarterly estimated tax payments.

For workers, whether employee or independent contractor status is more beneficial depends on many factors including the extent to which an independent contractor is able to negotiate for gross payments that include the value of nonwage costs that the service provider would have to incur in the case of an employee. In some circumstances, independent contractor status is more beneficial; in other circumstances, employee status is more advantageous.

Under a special provision (section 530 of the Revenue Act of 1978 which was not made part of the Internal Revenue Code), a service recipient may treat a worker as an independent contractor for Federal employment tax purposes even though the worker actually may be an employee under the common law rules if the service recipient has a reasonable basis for treating the worker as an independent contractor and certain other requirements are met. The special provision applies only if (1) the service recipient has not treated the worker (or any worker in a substantially similar position) as an employee for any period beginning after 1977 and (2) the service recipient has filed all Federal tax returns, including all required information returns, on a basis consistent with treating the worker as an independent contractor.

If an employer meets the requirements for the special provision with respect to a class of workers, the IRS is prohibited from reclassifying the workers as employees, even prospectively and even as to newly hired workers in the same class. Since 1996, the IRS has considered the availability of the special provision as the first part of any examination concerning worker classification. If the IRS determines that the special provision applies to a class of workers, it does not determine whether the workers are in fact employees or independent contractors. Thus, the worker classification continues indefinitely even if it is incorrect.

The special provision also prohibits the IRS from issuing generally applicable guidance addressing the proper classification of workers. Current law and procedures also provide for reduced penalties for misclassification where the special provision is not available but where, among other things, the employer agrees to prospective reclassification of the workers as employees.

Reasons for Change

Since 1978, the IRS has not been permitted to issue general guidance addressing worker classification, and in many instances has been precluded from reclassifying workers – even prospectively – who may have been misclassified. Since 1978 there have been many changes in working relationships between service providers and service recipients. As a result, there has been continued and growing uncertainty about the correct classification of some workers.

Many benefits and worker protections are available only for workers who are classified as employees. Incorrect classification as an independent contractor for tax purposes may spill over to other areas and, for example, lead to a worker not receiving benefits for unemployment (unemployment insurance) or on-the-job injuries (workers' compensation), or not being protected by various on-the-job health and safety requirements.

The incorrect classification of workers also creates opportunities for competitive advantages over service recipients who properly classify their workers. Such misclassification may lower the service recipient's total cost of labor by avoiding workers' compensation and unemployment compensation premiums, and could also provide increased opportunities for noncompliance by service providers.

Workers, service recipients, and tax administrators would benefit from reducing uncertainty about worker classification, eliminating potential competitive advantages and incentives to misclassify workers associated with worker misclassification by competitors, and reducing opportunities for noncompliance by workers classified as self-employed, while maintaining the benefits and worker protections associated with an administrative and social policy system that is based on employee status.

Proposal

The proposal would permit the IRS to require prospective reclassification of workers who are currently misclassified and whose reclassification has been prohibited under current law. The reduced penalties for misclassification provided under current law would be retained, except that lower penalties would apply only if the service recipient voluntarily reclassifies its workers before being contacted by the IRS or another enforcement agency and if the service recipient had filed all required information returns (Forms 1099) reporting the payments to the independent contractors. For service recipients with only a small number of employees and a small number of misclassified workers, even reduced penalties would be waived if the service recipient (1) had consistently filed Forms 1099 reporting all payments to all misclassified workers and (2) agreed to prospective reclassification of misclassified workers. It is anticipated that, after enactment, new enforcement activity would focus mainly on obtaining the proper worker classification prospectively, since in many cases the proper classification of workers may not have been clear. (Statutory employee or nonemployee treatment as specified under current law would be retained.)

The Department of the Treasury and the IRS also would be permitted to issue generally applicable guidance on the proper classification of workers under common law standards. This would enable service recipients to properly classify workers with much less concern about future IRS examinations. Treasury and the IRS would be directed to issue guidance interpreting common law in a neutral manner recognizing that many workers are, in fact, not employees. Further, Treasury and the IRS would develop guidance that would provide safe harbors and/or rebuttable presumptions, both narrowly defined. To make that guidance clearer and more useful for service recipients, it would generally be industry- or job-specific. Priority for the development of guidance would be given to industries and jobs in which application of the common law test has been particularly problematic, where there has been a history of worker misclassification, or where there have been failures to report compensation paid.

Service recipients would be required to give notice to independent contractors, when they first begin performing services for the service recipient, that explains how they will be classified and the consequences thereof, e.g., tax implications, workers' compensation implications, wage and hour implications.

The IRS would be permitted to disclose to the Department of Labor information about service recipients whose workers are reclassified.

To ease compliance burdens for independent contractors, independent contractors receiving payments totaling $600 or more in a calendar year from a service recipient would be permitted to require the service recipient to withhold for Federal tax purposes a flat rate percentage of their gross payments, with the flat rate percentage being selected by the contractor.

The proposal would be effective upon enactment, but prospective reclassification of those covered by the current special provision would not be effective until the first calendar year beginning at least one year after date of enactment. The transition period could be up to two years for independent contractors with existing written contracts establishing their status.

REPEAL SPECIAL ESTIMATED TAX PAYMENT PROVISION FOR CERTAIN INSURANCE COMPANIES

Current Law

An insurance company uses reserve accounting to compute losses incurred. That is, losses incurred for the taxable year includes losses paid during the taxable year (net of salvage and reinsurance recovered), plus or minus the increase or decrease in discounted unpaid losses during the year. An adjustment is also made for the change in discounted estimated salvage and reinsurance recoverable.

Unpaid losses are determined on a discounted basis to account for the time that may elapse between an insured loss event and the payment or other resolution of the claim. Taxpayers may, however, elect under section 847 to take an additional deduction equal to the difference between the amount of their reserves computed on a discounted basis and the amount computed on an undiscounted basis. In order to do so, a taxpayer must make a special estimated tax payment (SETP) equal to the tax benefit attributable to the additional deduction. In addition, the additional deductions are added to a special loss discount account. In future years, as losses are paid, amounts are subtracted from the special discount account and included in gross income; the SETPs are used to offset tax generated by these income inclusions. To the extent an amount added to the special loss discount account is not subtracted within 15 years, it is automatically subtracted (and included in gross income) for the 15th year. This regime of additional deductions and SETPs is, by design, revenue neutral.

Reasons for Change

Although this provision is revenue neutral, it imposes a substantial recordkeeping burden on both taxpayers and the Internal Revenue Service. Records must be maintained for up to 15 years for both amounts added to the special loss discount account and amounts paid as SETPs. Additional complexities frequently arise, such as when a taxpayer has a net operating loss carryback, or when a taxpayer is subject to regular tax in one year and alternative minimum tax in another. Also, further complexity arises under section 847 because an insurance company must account for tax benefits that would arise from the filing of a consolidated return with other insurance companies without taking into account statutory limitations on the absorption of losses of non-life insurers against income of life insurance companies.

Proposal

The proposal would repeal section 847 of the Internal Revenue Code, effective for taxable years beginning after December 31, 2011.

The entire balance of any existing special loss discount account would be included in gross income for the first taxable year beginning after December 31, 2011, and the entire amount of existing SETPs would be applied against additional tax that is due as a result of that inclusion. Any SETPs in excess of the additional tax that is due would be treated as an estimated tax payment under section 6655.

In lieu of immediate inclusion in gross income for the first taxable year beginning after December 31, 2011, taxpayers would be permitted to elect to include the balance of any existing special loss discount account in gross income ratably over a four taxable year period, beginning with the first taxable year beginning after December 31, 2011. During this period, taxpayers would be permitted to use existing SETPs to offset any additional tax that is due as a result of that inclusion. At the end of the fourth year, any remaining SETPs would be treated as an estimated tax payment under section 6655.

ELIMINATE SPECIAL RULES MODIFYING THE AMOUNT OF ESTIMATED TAX PAYMENTS BY CORPORATIONS

Current Law

Under section 6655 of the Internal Revenue Code, corporations generally are required to pay their income tax liability for a taxable year in quarterly estimated payments. For corporations that keep their accounts on a calendar year basis, these payments are generally due on or before April 15, June 15, September 15 and December 15 of the particular taxable year. The amount due each quarter is generally one-quarter (25 percent) of the amount due for the year.

A number of acts have modified the standard rules as to the amount due by "large corporations" for a particular quarter. A large corporation, for this purpose, means a corporation with assets of $1 billion or more, determined as of the end of the preceding taxable year. For example, Public Law 111-210, which renewed import restrictions under the Burmese Freedom and Democracy Act of 2003, increased the quarterly estimated tax payment required by large corporations for July, August or September, 2015, to 121.75 percent of the amount otherwise due. Where the amount required for a particular quarter has been increased, the amount of the next required quarterly payment is reduced accordingly.

Reasons for Change

The frequent changes to the corporate estimated tax payment schedule do not generally increase a corporation's income tax liability for a particular taxable year. However, the frequency of such changes operates to increase uncertainty within the corporate tax system.

Proposal

The proposal would repeal all legislative acts that cause the amount and timing of corporate estimated payments to differ from the rules described under section 6655.

The proposal would be effective for taxable years beginning after December 31, 2011.

Strengthen Tax Administration

REVISE OFFER-IN-COMPROMISE APPLICATION RULES

Current Law

Current law provides that the Internal Revenue Service (IRS) may compromise any civil or criminal case arising under the internal revenue laws prior to a reference to the Department of Justice for prosecution or defense. In 2006, a new provision was enacted to require taxpayers to make certain nonrefundable payments with any initial offer-in-compromise of a tax case. The new provision requires taxpayers making a lump-sum offer-in-compromise to include a nonrefundable payment of 20 percent of the lump-sum with the initial offer. In the case of an offer-in-compromise involving periodic payments, the initial offer must be accompanied by a nonrefundable payment of the first installment that would be due if the offer were accepted.

Reasons for Change

Requiring nonrefundable payments with an offer-in-compromise may substantially reduce access to the offer-in-compromise program. The offer-in-compromise program is designed to settle cases in which taxpayers have demonstrated an inability to pay the full amount of a tax liability. The program allows the IRS to collect the portion of a tax liability that the taxpayer has the ability to pay. Reducing access to the offer-in-compromise program makes it more difficult and costly to obtain the collectable portion of existing tax liabilities.

Proposal

The proposal would eliminate the requirements that an initial offer-in-compromise include a nonrefundable payment of any portion of the taxpayer's offer.

The proposal would be effective for offers-in-compromise submitted after the date of enactment.

EXPAND INTERNAL REVENUE SERVICE (IRS) ACCESS TO INFORMATION IN THE NATIONAL DIRECTORY OF NEW HIRES FOR TAX ADMINISTRATION PURPOSES

Current Law

The Office of Child Support Enforcement of the Department of Health and Human Services maintains the National Directory of New Hires (NDNH), which is a database that contains data from Form W-4 for newly-hired employees, quarterly wage data from State workforce and Federal agencies for all employees, and unemployment insurance data from State workforce agencies for all individuals who have applied for or received unemployment benefits. The NDNH was created to help State child support enforcement agencies enforce obligations of parents across State lines.

Under current provisions of the Social Security Act, the IRS may obtain data from the NDNH, but only for the purpose of administering the earned income tax credit (EITC) and verifying employment reported on a tax return.

Generally, the IRS obtains employment and unemployment data less frequently than quarterly, and there are significant internal costs of preparing these data for use. Under various State laws, the IRS may negotiate for access to employment and unemployment data directly from State agencies that maintain these data.

Reasons for Change

Employment data are useful to the IRS in administering a wide range of tax provisions beyond the EITC, including verifying taxpayer claims and identifying levy sources. Currently, the IRS may obtain employment and unemployment data on a State-by-State basis, which is a costly and time-consuming process. NDNH data are timely, uniformly compiled, and electronically accessible. Access to the NDNH would increase the productivity of the IRS by reducing the amount of IRS resources dedicated to obtaining and processing data without reducing the current levels of taxpayer privacy.

Proposal

The proposal would amend the Social Security Act to expand IRS access to NDNH data for general tax administration purposes, including data matching, verification of taxpayer claims during return processing, preparation of substitute returns for non-compliant taxpayers, and identification of levy sources. Data obtained by the IRS from the NDNH would be protected by existing taxpayer privacy law, including civil and criminal sanctions.

The proposal would be effective upon enactment.

MAKE REPEATED WILLFUL FAILURE TO FILE A TAX RETURN A FELONY

Current Law

Current law provides that willful failure to file a tax return is a misdemeanor punishable by a term of imprisonment for not more than one year, a fine of not more than $25,000 ($100,000 in the case of a corporation), or both. A taxpayer who fails to file returns for multiple years commits a separate misdemeanor offense for each year.

Reasons for Change

Increased criminal penalties would help to deter multiple willful failures to file tax returns.

Proposal

The proposal would provide that any person who willfully fails to file tax returns in any three years within any five consecutive year period, if the aggregated tax liability for such period is at least $50,000, would be subject to a new aggravated failure to file criminal penalty. The proposal would classify such failure as a felony and, upon conviction, impose a fine of not more than $250,000 ($500,000 in the case of a corporation) or imprisonment for not more than five years, or both.

The proposal would be effective for returns required to be filed after December 31, 2011.

FACILITATE TAX COMPLIANCE WITH LOCAL JURISDICTIONS

Current Law

Although Federal tax returns and return information (FTI) generally are confidential, the Internal Revenue Service (IRS) and Treasury Department may share FTI with States as well as certain local government entities that are treated as States for this purpose. Generally, the purpose of information sharing is to facilitate tax administration. Where sharing of FTI is authorized, reciprocal provisions generally authorize disclosure of information to the IRS by State and local governments. State and local governments that receive FTI must safeguard it according to prescribed protocols that require secure storage, restricted access, reports to IRS, and shredding or other proper disposal. See, e.g., IRS Publication 1075. Criminal and civil sanctions apply to unauthorized disclosure or inspection of FTI. Indian Tribal Governments (ITGs) are treated as States by the tax law for several purposes, such as certain charitable contributions, excise tax credits, and local tax deductions, but not for purposes of information sharing.

Reasons for Change

IRS and Treasury compliance activity, especially with respect to alcohol, tobacco and fuel excise taxes, may necessitate information sharing with ITGs. For example, the IRS may wish to confirm if a fuel supplier's claim to have delivered particular amounts to adjacent jurisdictions is consistent with that reported to the IRS. If not, the IRS in conjunction with the ITG, which would have responsibility for administering taxes imposed by the ITG, can take steps to ensure compliance with both Federal and ITG tax laws. Where the local government is treated as a State for information sharing purposes, IRS, Treasury, and local officials can support each other's efforts. Where the local government is not so treated, there is an impediment to compliance activity.

Proposal

For purposes of information sharing, the proposal would treat as States those ITGs that impose alcohol, tobacco, or fuel excise or income or wage taxes, to the extent necessary for ITG tax administration. An ITG that receives FTI would be required to safeguard it according to prescribed protocols. The criminal and civil sanctions would apply.

The proposal would be effective for disclosures made after enactment.

EXTEND STATUTE OF LIMITATIONS WHERE STATE ADJUSTMENT AFFECTS FEDERAL TAX LIABILITY

Current Law

In general, additional Federal tax liabilities in the form of tax, interest, penalties and additions to tax must be assessed by the Internal Revenue Service (IRS) within three years after the date a return is filed. If an assessment is not made within the required time period, the additional liabilities generally cannot be assessed or collected at any future time. In general, the statute of limitations with respect to claims for refund expires three years from the time the return was filed or two years from the time the tax was paid, whichever is later. The Code contains exceptions to the general statute of limitations.

State and local authorities employ a variety of statutes of limitations for State and local tax assessments. Pursuant to agreement, the IRS and State and local revenue agencies exchange reports of adjustments made through examination so that corresponding adjustments can be made by each taxing authority. In addition, States provide the IRS with reports of potential discrepancies between State returns and Federal returns.

Reasons for Change

The general statute of limitations serves as a barrier to the effective use by the IRS of State and local tax adjustment reports when the reports are provided by the State or local revenue agency to the IRS with little time remaining for assessments to be made at the Federal level. Under the current statute of limitations framework, taxpayers may seek to extend the State statute of limitations or postpone agreement to State proposed adjustments until such time as the Federal statute of limitations expires in order to preclude assessment at the Federal level. In addition, it is not always the case that a taxpayer that files an amended State or local return reporting additional liabilities at the State or local level that also affect Federal tax liability will file an amended return at the Federal level.

Proposal

The proposal would create an additional exception to the general three-year statute of limitations for assessment of Federal tax liability resulting from adjustments to State or local tax liability. The statute of limitations would be extended to the greater of: (1) one year from the date the taxpayer first files an amended tax return with the IRS reflecting adjustments to the State or local tax return; or (2) two years from the date the IRS first receives information from the State or local revenue agency under an information sharing agreement in place between the IRS and a State or local revenue agency. The statute of limitations would be extended only with respect to the increase in Federal tax attributable to the State or local tax adjustment. The statute of limitations would not be further extended if the taxpayer files additional amended returns for the same tax periods as the initial amended return or if the IRS receives additional information from the State or local revenue agency under an information sharing agreement. The statute of limitations on claims for refund would be extended correspondingly so that any overall increase in tax assessed by the IRS as a result of the State or local examination report would take into account agreed-upon tax decreases or reductions attributable to a refund or credit.

The proposal would be effective for returns required to be filed after December 31, 2011.

IMPROVE INVESTIGATIVE DISCLOSURE STATUTE

Current Law

Generally, tax return information is confidential, unless a specific exception in the Code applies. In the case of tax administration, the Code permits Treasury and Internal Revenue Service (IRS) officers and employees to disclose return information to the extent necessary to obtain information not otherwise reasonably available, in the course of an audit or investigation, as prescribed by regulation. Thus, for example, a revenue agent may identify himself or herself as affiliated with the IRS, and may disclose the nature and subject of an investigation, as necessary to elicit information from a witness in connection with that investigation. Criminal and civil sanctions apply to unauthorized disclosures of return information.

Reasons for Change

Treasury Regulations effective since 2003 state that the term "necessary" in this context does not mean essential or indispensable, but rather appropriate and helpful in obtaining the information sought. In other contexts, a "necessary" disclosure is one without which performance cannot be accomplished reasonably without the disclosure. Determining if an investigative disclosure is "necessary" is inherently factual, leading to inconsistent opinions by the courts. Eliminating this uncertainty from the statute would facilitate investigations by IRS officers and employees, while setting forth clear guidance for taxpayers, thus enhancing compliance with the tax Code.

Proposal

The proposal would clarify the taxpayer privacy law by stating that the law does not prohibit Treasury and IRS officers and employees from identifying themselves, their organizational affiliation, and the nature and subject of an investigation, when contacting third parties in connection with a civil or criminal tax investigation.

The proposal would be effective for disclosures made after enactment.

REQUIRE TAXPAYERS WHO PREPARE THEIR RETURNS ELECTRONICALLY BUT FILE THEIR RETURNS ON PAPER TO PRINT THEIR RETURNS WITH A 2-D BAR CODE

Current Law

Taxpayers can prepare their tax returns electronically (either by utilizing a tax return preparer or using tax return software at home) and, instead of filing their returns electronically, may print out a paper copy and file the return on paper by mailing it to the Internal Revenue Service (IRS).

Reasons for Change

Electronically filed tax returns are processed more efficiently and more accurately than paper tax returns. When tax returns are filed on paper—even if that paper return was prepared electronically—the IRS is unable to scan the return and the information contained on the return must be manually entered into the IRS's systems.

New scanning technology would allow the IRS to scan paper tax returns and capture all data shown on the return, if the paper return contains a 2-D bar code that would allow conversion of the paper return into an electronic format. This would reduce the amount of training, recruiting, and staffing that the IRS requires to process paper tax returns. In addition, the IRS would have greater access to more accurate tax data, thereby improving case selection, assisting in the detection of fraudulent tax returns, and allowing more comprehensive analysis of taxpayer behavior.

Proposal

The proposal would require all taxpayers who prepare their tax returns electronically but print their returns and file them on paper to print their returns with a 2-D bar code that can be scanned by the IRS to convert the paper return into an electronic format.

The proposal would be effective for tax returns filed after December 31, 2011.

REQUIRE PRISONS LOCATED IN THE U.S. TO PROVIDE INFORMATION TO THE INTERNAL REVENUE SERVICE (IRS)

Current Law

The IRS is unable to cross reference tax returns received with a list of prison inmates to determine whether inmates are claiming tax benefits to which they are not entitled.

Reasons for Change

The IRS has become aware that some incarcerated individuals are claiming tax benefits to which they may not be entitled. For example, some inmates file false returns claiming a refund, based upon false W-2 statements created by the inmate showing that the inmate has earned income from a legitimate business and that taxes were withheld on that income. Some inmates claim the earned income tax credit (EITC), even though section 32 provides that no income for services provided while the individual is an inmate at a penal institution shall be taken into account for purposes of the EITC.

By requiring that all inmates' names and validated Social Security numbers be provided to the IRS, the IRS could cross reference tax returns with the list of inmates to determine if a legitimate return is filed, before tax refunds are paid. Although the IRS is working with state and federal prison systems to collect information on the prison population, the IRS is currently unable to consistently identify tax returns filed by prisoners and may not be able to immediately determine that income could not have been earned outside of the institution where the inmate was incarcerated.

Proposal

The proposal would require all prisons located in the United States to submit to the IRS by December 1 of each year a list of names and validated Social Security numbers of all inmates serving sentences of one year or more.

The proposal would be effective upon enactment.

ALLOW THE INTERNAL REVENUE SERVICE (IRS) TO ABSORB CREDIT AND DEBIT CARD PROCESSING FEES FOR CERTAIN TAX PAYMENTS

Current Law

Section 6311 permits the IRS to receive payment of taxes by any commercially acceptable means that the Secretary deems appropriate. Taxpayers may make credit or debit card payments by phone through IRS-designated third party service providers, but these providers charge the taxpayer a convenience fee over and above the taxes due. Taxpayers cannot make a credit or debit card payment by phone directly to IRS collection representatives. Under current law, if the IRS were to accept credit or debit card payments directly from taxpayers, the IRS is prohibited from absorbing credit or debit card processing fees.

Reasons for Change

When taxpayers agree to make additional payments during in telephone consultations with IRS agents, it is inefficient for both taxpayers and the IRS to require taxpayers to contact a third party service provider to make credit and debit card payments. Both the requirement for a separate call to a service provider and the additional processing fee for such payments may also discourage payment of outstanding liabilities, resulting in greater collection costs for the IRS, fewer IRS resources available to contact additional taxpayers, and lower tax collections. Allowing IRS to accept credit and debit card payments directly and allowing the IRS to absorb the credit and debit card processing fees would increase efficiency and the number of collection cases worked. Permitting the IRS to absorb the processing fee would increase payment options available to taxpayers.

Proposal

The proposal would amend Section 6311(d) to allow the IRS to accept credit or debit card payments directly from taxpayers and to absorb the credit and debit card processing fees for certain tax payments, without charging a separate processing fee to the taxpayer.

The proposal would be effective for payments made after the date of enactment.

Expand Penalties

IMPOSE A PENALTY ON FAILURE TO COMPLY WITH ELECTRONIC FILING REQUIREMENTS

Current Law

Certain corporations and tax-exempt organizations (including certain charitable trusts and private foundations) are required to file their returns electronically. Generally, filing on paper instead of electronically is treated as a failure to file if electronic filing is required. Additions to tax are imposed for the failure to file tax returns reporting a liability. For failure to file a corporate return, the addition to tax is 5 percent of the amount required to be shown as tax due on the return, for the first month of failure, and an additional 5 percent for each month or part of a month thereafter, up to a maximum of 25 percent.

For failure to file a tax-exempt organization return, the addition to tax is $20 a day for each day the failure continues. The maximum amount per return is $10,000 or 5 percent of the organization's gross receipts for the year, whichever is less. Organizations with annual gross receipts exceeding $1 million, however, are subject to an addition to tax of $100 per day, with a maximum of $50,000.

Reasons for Change

Although there are additions to tax for the failure to file returns, there is no specific penalty for a failure to comply with a requirement to file electronically. Because the addition to tax for failure to file a corporate return is based on an underpayment of tax, no addition is imposed if the corporation is in a refund, credit, or loss status. Thus, the existing addition to tax may not provide an adequate incentive for certain corporations to file electronically. Generally, electronic filing increases efficiency of tax administration because the provision of tax return information in an electronic form enables the Internal Revenue Service to focus audit activities where they can have the greatest impact. This also assists taxpayers where the need for audit is reduced.

Proposal

The proposal would establish an assessable penalty for a failure to comply with a requirement of electronic (or other machine-readable) format for a return that is filed. The amount of the penalty would be $25,000 for a corporation or $5,000 for a tax-exempt organization. For failure to file in any format, the existing penalty would remain, and the proposed penalty would not apply.

The proposal would be effective for returns required to be electronically filed after December 31, 2011.

INCREASE PENALTY IMPOSED ON PAID PREPARERS WHO FAIL TO COMPLY WITH EARNED INCOME TAX CREDIT (EITC) DUE DILIGENCE REQUIREMENTS

Current Law

Section 6695(g) imposes a $100 penalty on tax return preparers who fail to comply with the due diligence requirements imposed by regulations with respect to determining eligibility for, or the amount of, the EITC for each such failure.

Reasons for Change

The Internal Revenue Service estimates that as many as a quarter of EITC claims are made in error. Since more than two-thirds of EITC claims are prepared by paid tax return preparers, tax return preparers can have a substantial impact on reducing the number of errors in EITC claims. Increasing the due diligence penalty amount, which has not been adjusted since the penalty was introduced in 1997, will help ensure that preparers comply with the due diligence requirements.

Proposal

The proposal would increase the Section 6695(g) penalty from $100 to $500.

The proposal would be effective for returns required to be filed after December 31, 2011.

Modify Estate and Gift Tax Valuation Discounts and Make Other Reforms

MAKE PERMANENT THE PORTABILITY OF UNUSED EXEMPTION BETWEEN SPOUSES

Current Law

Each individual has a lifetime exclusion for purposes of estate and gift taxes. That exclusion is $5 million in 2011 and will be indexed for inflation after 2011. However, after 2012, the amount of this exclusion is scheduled to revert to the amount that would have been in effect had the Economic Growth and Tax Relief Reconciliation Act of 2001 (EGTRRA) never been enacted (thus, $1 million). For the first time, current law now provides that the surviving spouse of a person who dies after December 31, 2010, may be eligible to increase the surviving spouse's exclusion amount by the portion of the predeceased spouse's exclusion that remained unused at the predeceased spouse's death. In no event, however, may the surviving spouse's exclusion amount be increased by more than the amount of exclusion available to a person in that calendar year. This provision allowing the portability of the predeceased spouse's unused exemption applies through December 31, 2012. If a surviving spouse is predeceased by more than one spouse, the amount of unused exclusion that is available for use by such surviving spouse is limited to the unused exclusion of the last such deceased spouse to die. The surviving spouse may use his or her exclusion, augmented by such predeceased spouse's unused exclusion, for taxable transfers made during life or at death.

The surviving spouse may use the unused exclusion of such predeceased spouse only if the executor of that predeceased spouse makes an election on a timely filed estate tax return (including extensions) for the estate of that predeceased spouse on which such unused exemption amount is computed, regardless of whether the estate of that predeceased spouse otherwise is required to file an estate tax return. Notwithstanding the statute of limitations for assessing estate or gift tax with respect to that predeceased spouse, the return of that predeceased spouse may be examined and adjusted for purposes of determining the deceased spouse's unused exclusion amount available for use by the surviving spouse.

Reasons for Change

Without this portability provision, spouses are often required to retitle assets into each spouse's separate name and create complex trusts in order to allow the first spouse to die to take full advantage of his or her exclusion. Depending upon the nature of the couple's assets, such a division may not be possible. Such a division also has significant consequences under property law and often is not consistent with the way in which the married couple would prefer to handle their financial affairs. Portability would obviate the need for such burdensome planning.

Proposal

This proposal would extend portability permanently, thus making the use of the last predeceased spouse's unused exemption available to all estates of decedents dying and gifts made after December 31, 2012.

REQUIRE CONSISTENCY IN VALUE FOR TRANSFER AND INCOME TAX PURPOSES

Current Law

Section 1014 provides that the basis of property acquired from a decedent generally is the fair market value of the property on the decedent's date of death. Similarly, property included in the decedent's gross estate for estate tax purposes generally must be valued at its fair market value on the date of death. Although the same valuation standard applies to both provisions, current law does not explicitly require that the recipient's basis in that property be the same as the value at which that property was reported for estate tax purposes.

Section 1015 provides that the donee's basis in property received by gift during the life of the donor generally is the donor's adjusted basis in the property, increased by gift tax paid on the transfer. If, however, the donor's basis exceeds the fair market value of the property on the date of the gift, the donee's basis is limited to that fair market value for purposes of determining any subsequent loss.

Section 1022, applicable to the estates of decedents dying during 2010 if a timely election to that effect is made, provides that the basis of property acquired from such a decedent is the lesser of the decedent's adjusted basis in that property or the fair market value of the property on the decedent's date of death.

Section 6034A imposes a consistency requirement – specifically, that the recipient of a distribution of income from a trust or estate must report on the recipient's own income tax return the exact information included on the Schedule K-1 of the trust's or estate's income tax return – but this provision applies only for income tax purposes, and the Schedule K-1 does not include basis information.

Reasons for Change

Taxpayers should be required to take consistent positions in dealing with the Internal Revenue Service, whether or not principles of privity apply. If the logic underlying the determination of the new basis in property acquired on the death of the owner is that the new basis is the amount used to determine the decedent's estate tax liability, then the law should require that the same value be used by the recipient, unless that value is in excess of the accurate value. In the case of property transferred on death or by gift during life, often the executor of the estate or the donor, respectively, will be in the best position to ensure that the recipient receives the information that will be necessary to determine the recipient's basis in the transferred property.

Proposal

This proposal would impose both a consistency and a reporting requirement. The basis of property received by reason of death under section 1014 must equal the value of that property for estate tax purposes. The basis of property received by gift during the life of the donor must equal the donor's basis determined under section 1015. The basis of property acquired from a decedent to whose estate section 1022 is applicable is the lesser of the decedent's adjusted basis or the fair market value of the property on the decedent's death. This proposal would require that the basis of the property in the hands of the recipient be no greater than the value of that property as determined for estate or gift tax purposes (subject to subsequent adjustments).

A reporting requirement would be imposed on the executor of the decedent's estate and on the donor of a lifetime gift to provide the necessary valuation information to both the recipient and the Internal Revenue Service.

A grant of regulatory authority would be included to provide details about the implementation and administration of these requirements, including rules for situations in which no estate tax return is required to be filed or gifts are excluded from gift tax under section 2503, for situations in which the surviving joint tenant or other recipient may have better information than the executor, and for the timing of the required reporting in the event of adjustments to the reported value subsequent to the filing of an estate or gift tax return.

The proposal would be effective as of the date of enactment.

MODIFY RULES ON VALUATION DISCOUNTS

Current Law

The fair market value of property transferred, whether on the death or during the life of the transferor, generally is subject to estate or gift tax at the time of the transfer. Sections 2701 through 2704 of the Internal Revenue Code were enacted to prevent the reduction of taxes through the use of "estate freezes" and other techniques designed to reduce the value of the transferor's taxable estate and discount the value of the taxable transfer to the beneficiaries of the transferor without reducing the economic benefit to the beneficiaries. Generally, section 2704(b) provides that certain "applicable restrictions" (that would normally justify discounts in the value of the interests transferred) are to be ignored in valuing interests in family-controlled entities if those interests are transferred (either by gift or on death) to or for the benefit of other family members. The application of these special rules results in an increase in the transfer tax value of those interests above the price that a hypothetical willing buyer would pay a willing seller, because section 2704(b) generally directs an appraiser to ignore the rights and restrictions that otherwise would support significant discounts for lack of marketability and control.

Reasons for Change

Judicial decisions and the enactment of new statutes in most states, in effect, have made section 2704(b) inapplicable in many situations by recharacterizing restrictions such that they no longer fall within the definition of an "applicable restriction". In addition, the Internal Revenue Service has identified additional arrangements designed to circumvent the application of section 2704.

Proposal

This proposal would create an additional category of restrictions ("disregarded restrictions") that would be ignored in valuing an interest in a family-controlled entity transferred to a member of the family if, after the transfer, the restriction will lapse or may be removed by the transferor and/or the transfer's family. Specifically, the transferred interest would be valued by substituting for the disregarded restrictions certain assumptions to be specified in regulations. Disregarded restrictions would include limitations on a holder's right to liquidate that holder's interest that are more restrictive than a standard to be identified in regulations. A disregarded restriction also would include any limitation on a transferee's ability to be admitted as a full partner or to hold an equity interest in the entity. For purposes of determining whether a restriction may be removed by member(s) of the family after the transfer, certain interests (to be identified in regulations) held by charities or others who are not family members of the transferor would be deemed to be held by the family. Regulatory authority would be granted, including the ability to create safe harbors to permit taxpayers to draft the governing documents of a family-controlled entity so as to avoid the application of section 2704 if certain standards are met. This proposal would make conforming clarifications with regard to the interaction of this proposal with the transfer tax marital and charitable deductions.

This proposal would apply to transfers after the date of enactment of property subject to restrictions created after October 8, 1990 (the effective date of section 2704).

REQUIRE A MINIMUM TERM FOR GRANTOR RETAINED ANNUITY TRUSTS (GRATS)

Current Law

Section 2702 provides that, if an interest in a trust is transferred to a family member, the value of any interest retained by the grantor is valued at zero for purposes of determining the transfer tax value of the gift to the family member(s). This rule does not apply if the retained interest is a "qualified interest." A fixed annuity, such as the annuity interest retained by the grantor of a GRAT, is one form of qualified interest, so the gift of the remainder interest in the GRAT is determined by deducting the present value of the retained annuity during the GRAT term from the fair market value of the property contributed to the trust.

Generally, a GRAT is an irrevocable trust funded with assets expected to appreciate in value, in which the grantor retains an annuity interest for a term of years that the grantor expects to survive. At the end of that term, the assets then remaining in the trust are transferred to (or held in further trust for) the beneficiaries, who generally are descendants of the grantor. If the grantor dies during the GRAT term, however, the trust assets (at least the portion needed to produce the retained annuity) are included in the grantor's gross estate for estate tax purposes. To this extent, although the beneficiaries will own the remaining trust assets, the estate tax benefit of creating the GRAT (specifically, the tax-free transfer of the appreciation during the GRAT term in excess of the annuity payments) is not realized.

Reasons for Change

GRATs have proven to be a popular and efficient technique for transferring wealth while minimizing the gift tax cost of transfers, providing that the grantor survives the GRAT term and the trust assets do not depreciate in value. The greater the appreciation, the greater the transfer tax benefit achieved. Taxpayers have become adept at maximizing the benefit of this technique, often by minimizing the term of the GRAT (thus reducing the risk of the grantor's death during the term), in many cases to two years, and by retaining annuity interests significant enough to reduce the gift tax value of the remainder interest to zero or to a number small enough to generate only a minimal gift tax liability.

Proposal

This proposal would require, in effect, some downside risk in the use of this technique by imposing the requirement that a GRAT have a minimum term of ten years.[9] The proposal would also include a requirement that the remainder interest have a value greater than zero and would prohibit any decrease in the annuity during the GRAT term. Although a minimum term would not prevent "zeroing-out" the gift tax value of the remainder interest, it would increase the risk of the grantor's death during the GRAT term and the resulting loss of any anticipated transfer tax benefit.

This proposal would apply to trusts created after the date of enactment.

---

[9] Cf. section 673 as applicable to a so-called *Clifford* trust created before or on March 1, 1986, with a ten-year minimum term.

LIMIT DURATION OF GENERATION-SKIPPING TRANSFER (GST) TAX EXEMPTION

Current Law

Generation-skipping transfer tax is imposed on gifts and bequests to transferees who are two or more generations younger than the transferor. The GST tax was enacted to "backstop" the estate and gift tax system by preventing the avoidance of those taxes through the use of a trust that gives successive life interests to multiple generations of beneficiaries. In such a trust, no estate tax would be incurred as beneficiaries died because their respective life interests would die with them and thus would cause no inclusion of the trust assets in the deceased beneficiary's gross estate. The GST tax is a flat tax on the value of the transfer at the highest estate tax bracket applicable in that year. Each person has a GST tax exemption (originally $1 million, $3.5 million in 2009, and $5 million in 2010 and 2011), that can be allocated to transfers made by that person, whether made directly to a grandchild or other "skip person" or in trust. The allocation of GST exemption to a transfer or to a trust excludes from the GST tax not only the amount of the transfer or trust assets equal to the amount of GST exemption allocated, but also all appreciation and income on that amount during the existence of the trust.

At the time of the enactment of the GST provisions, the law of most (generally, all but about three) states included the common law Rule against Perpetuities (RAP) or some statutory enactment or version of it. The RAP generally requires that every trust terminate no later than 21 years after the death of a person who was alive (a life in being) at the time of the creation of the trust.

Reasons for Change

Many states have now either repealed or limited the application of their RAP statutes, with the effect that trusts created subject to the law of those jurisdictions may continue in perpetuity. (A trust may be sitused anywhere; a grantor is not limited to the jurisdiction of the grantor's domicile for this purpose.) As a result, the transfer tax shield provided by the GST exemption effectively has been expanded from trusts funded with $1 million and a maximum duration limited by the RAP, to trusts funded with $5 million and continuing (and growing) in perpetuity.

Proposal

This proposal would provide that, on the 90th anniversary of the creation of a trust, the GST exclusion allocated to the trust would terminate. Specifically, this would be achieved by increasing the inclusion ratio of the trust (as defined in section 2642) to one, thereby rendering no part of the trust exempt from GST tax. Because contributions to a trust from a different grantor are deemed to be held in a separate trust under section 2654(b), each such separate trust would be subject to the same 90-year rule, measured from the date of the first contribution by the grantor of that separate trust. The special rule for pour-over trusts under section 2653(b)(2) would continue to apply to pour-over trusts and to trusts created under a decanting authority, and for purposes of this rule, such trusts will be deemed to have the same date of creation as the initial trust, with one exception, as follows. If, prior to the 90th anniversary of the trust, trust property is distributed to a trust for a beneficiary of the initial trust, and the distributee trust is as described in section 2642(c)(2), the inclusion ratio of the distributee trust will not be changed to one (with regard to the distribution from the initial trust) by reason of this rule. This exception is intended to permit an incapacitated beneficiary's distribution to continue to be held in trust without incurring GST tax on distributions to the beneficiary as long as that trust is to be used for the sole benefit of that beneficiary and any trust balance remaining on the beneficiary's death will be included in the beneficiary's gross estate for Federal estate tax purposes. The other rules of section 2653 also would continue to apply, and would be relevant in determining when a taxable distribution or taxable termination occurs after the 90th anniversary of the trust. An express grant of regulatory authority would be included to facilitate the implementation and administration of this provision.

This proposal would apply to trusts created after enactment, and to the portion of a pre-existing trust attributable to additions to such a trust made after that date (subject to rules substantially similar to the grandfather rules currently in effect for additions to trusts created prior to the effective date of the GST tax).

UPPER-INCOME TAX PROVISION

REDUCE THE VALUE OF CERTAIN TAX EXPENDITURES

Current Law

Under current law, individual taxpayers may elect to itemize their deductions instead of claiming a standard deduction. The allowable portion of an individual taxpayer's itemized deductions reduces the amount of taxable income. The value of (i.e., the reduction in tax from) the last dollar deducted is equal to the marginal tax rate multiplied times $1, e.g., if the marginal tax rate was 35 percent, then the value of the last dollar deducted would be 35 cents.

In general, itemized deductions include medical and dental expenses (in excess of 7.5 percent of adjusted gross income (AGI)[10]), state and local property taxes, either income or sales taxes, mortgage and investment interest paid, gifts to charities, casualty and theft losses (in excess of 10 percent of AGI), and job expenses and certain miscellaneous expenses (some only in excess of 2 percent of AGI).

For higher-income taxpayers, otherwise allowable itemized deductions (other than medical expenses, investment interest, theft and casualty losses, and gambling losses) were reduced prior to 2010 if AGI exceeded a statutory floor that was indexed annually for inflation. Prior to the enactment of the Economic Growth and Tax Relief Reconciliation Act of 2001 (EGTRRA), itemized deductions were reduced by 3 percent of AGI over the threshold, but not by more than 80 percent of the otherwise allowable deductions. EGTRRA reduced the itemized deduction limitation in three steps. For 2006 and 2007, itemized deductions were reduced by 2 percent of AGI over the threshold, but not by more than 53-1/3 percent. For 2008 and 2009, itemized deductions were reduced by 1 percent of AGI over the threshold, but not by more than 26-2/3 percent. For 2010, the reduction was completely eliminated. Under EGTRRA, the full itemized deduction reduction of 3 percent of AGI exceeding the floor (up to a maximum reduction of 80 percent of deductions), was scheduled to be reinstated in 2011. However, the Tax Relief, Unemployment Insurance Reauthorization, and Job Creation Act of 2010 extended the elimination of the itemized deduction reduction through 2012.

For 2011, the AGI floor, if it were applicable, would be $169,550 ($84,775 if married filing separately).

The Administration's modified PAYGO baseline assumes that in 2013 the income thresholds beyond which itemized deductions are reduced would be $250,000 for married taxpayers filing jointly and $200,000 for single taxpayers. The thresholds are expressed in 2009 dollars, and would be indexed for price inflation above the 2009 price level.

The Administration's baseline also assumes that the top individual income tax rate will be 35 percent through 2012, after which it will rise to 39.6 percent (see the description below of the modified PAYGO baseline).

---

[10] The AGI floor rises to 10 percent in 2013 for taxpayers under 65 years of age (2017 for all other taxpayers).

Reasons for Change

Increasing the income tax liability of higher-income taxpayers would reduce the deficit, make the income tax system more progressive, and distribute the cost of government more fairly among taxpayers of various income levels. In particular, capping the value of itemized deductions would reduce the benefit that high income taxpayers receive from the tax expenditures for the deduction of home mortgage interest, state and local property taxes, and charitable donations.

Proposal

This proposal would apply to itemized deductions after they have been reduced by the limitation on certain itemized deductions that is retained in the adjusted PAYGO baseline.

The proposal would further limit the value of all itemized deductions by limiting the tax value of otherwise allowable deductions to 28 percent for high income taxpayers. In 2012, the limitation would affect itemized deductions that would otherwise reduce taxable income in the 35 percent bracket and a portion of the 33 percent bracket. For 2013 and beyond the limitation would affect itemized deductions that would otherwise reduce taxable income in the 36 or 39.6 percent tax brackets. A similar limitation also would apply under the alternative minimum tax.

The proposal would be effective for taxable years beginning after December 31, 2011.

USER FEES

REFORM INLAND WATERWAYS FUNDING

Current Law

The Inland Waterways Trust Fund is authorized to pay 50 percent of the capital costs of the locks and dams that make commercial transportation possible on the inland and intracoastal waterways. This trust fund is supported by a 20-cents-per-gallon tax on liquids used as fuel in a vessel in commercial waterway transportation. Commercial waterway transportation is defined as any use of a vessel on a listed inland or intracoastal waterway of the United States: (1) in the business of transporting property for compensation or hire; or (2) in transporting property in the business of the owner, lessee, or operator of the vessel (other than fish or other aquatic animal life caught on the voyage). The inland or intracoastal waterways of the United States are the inland and intracoastal waterways of the United States described in section 206 of the Inland Waterways Revenue Act of 1978. Exceptions are provided for deep-draft ocean-going vessels, passenger vessels, State and local governments, and certain ocean-going barges.

Reasons for Change

The fuel excise tax does not raise enough revenue to pay the full amount of the authorized expenditures from this trust fund. Moreover, the tax is not the most efficient method for financing expenditures on those waterways. Sufficient funding can be provided through a more efficient user fee system that is based on lock usage and is tied to the level of spending for inland waterways construction, replacement, expansion, and rehabilitation work.

Proposal

One possible approach to the issue is a recent proposal by the Department of the Army (DOA). On behalf of the Administration, the DOA submitted a legislative proposal to the Congress in July 2009 under which the tax on liquids used as fuel in a vessel in commercial waterway transportation would be phased out and replaced by a fee system based on lock usage. Under an updated version of the 2009 proposal, the tax would be phased out and the fee system would be phased in as follows. The rate would be reduced to 10 cents per gallon beginning January 1, 2014 and would be repealed for periods after December 31, 2015. The fee system based on lock usage would be phased in beginning on October 1, 2012. For calendar year 2016 and each subsequent calendar year, the fee schedule would be adjusted as necessary to maintain an appropriate level of net assets in the Inland Waterways Trust Fund.

Based on the DOA proposal, or other sensible approaches, the Administration intends to work with the 112th Congress to reform the laws governing the Inland Waterways Trust Fund, including increasing the fees paid by commercial navigation users sufficiently to meet their share of the costs of activities financed from this trust fund.

OTHER INITIATIVES

ALLOW OFFSET OF FEDERAL INCOME TAX REFUNDS TO COLLECT DELINQUENT STATE INCOME TAXES FOR OUT-OF-STATE RESIDENTS

Current Law

Generally, the Treasury refunds a taxpayer who makes an overpayment (by withholding or otherwise) of Federal tax. The overpayment amount is reduced by (i.e., offset by) debts of the taxpayer for past-due child support, debts to Federal agencies, fraudulently obtained unemployment compensation, and past-due, legally enforceable State income tax obligations. In the latter case, a refund offset is permitted only if the delinquent taxpayer resides in the State seeking the offset.

Reasons for Change

Under current law, a delinquent taxpayer can escape offset of a Federal refund for a State tax liability as long as the taxpayer is not a resident of the State. Foreclosing this possibility would better leverage the capacity of the Federal tax refund offset program for the country as a whole.

Proposal

The proposal would permit offset of Federal refunds to collect State income tax, regardless of where the delinquent taxpayer resides.

The proposal would be effective on the date of enactment.

AUTHORIZE THE LIMITED SHARING OF BUSINESS TAX RETURN INFORMATION TO IMPROVE THE ACCURACY OF IMPORTANT MEASURES OF OUR ECONOMY

Current Law

Current law authorizes the Internal Revenue Service (IRS) to disclose certain federal tax information (FTI) for governmental statistical use. Business FTI may be disclosed to officers and employees of the Census Bureau for all businesses. Similarly, business FTI may be disclosed to officers and employees of the Bureau of Economic Analysis (BEA), but only for corporate businesses. Specific items permitted to be disclosed are detailed in the associated Treasury Regulations. The Bureau of Labor Statistics (BLS) is currently not authorized to receive FTI.

Reasons for Change

BEA's limited access to business FTI and BLS's lack of access to business FTI prevents BEA, Census, and BLS from synchronizing their business lists. Synchronization of business lists would significantly improve the consistency and quality of sensitive economic statistics including productivity, payroll, employment, and average hourly earnings.

In addition, given the growth of non-corporate businesses, especially in the service sector, the current limitation on BEA's access to corporate FTI impedes the measurement of income and international transactions in the National Accounts. The accuracy and consistency of income data are important to the formulation of fiscal policies.

Further, the Census's Business Register is constructed using both FTI and non-tax business data derived from the Economic Census and current economic surveys. Because this non-tax business data is inextricably co-mingled with FTI, it is not possible for Census to share data with BEA and BLS in any meaningful way.

Proposal

This proposal would give officers and employees of BEA access to FTI of those sole proprietorships with receipts greater than $250,000 and of all partnerships. BEA contractors would not have access to FTI.

This proposal would also give officers and employees of BLS access to certain business (and tax-exempt entities) FTI including: taxpayer identification number; name(s) of the business; business address (mailing address and physical location); principal industry activity (including business description); number of employees and total business-level wages (including wages, tips, and other compensation, quarterly from Form 941 and annually from Forms 943 and 944); and sales revenue for employer businesses only. BLS would not have access to individual employee FTI. Additionally, for the purpose of synchronizing BLS and Census business lists, the proposal would permit employees of state agencies to receive from BLS the following FTI identity items: taxpayer identification number, business name(s), business address(es), and principal industry activity (including business description). No BLS contractor or State agency contractor would have access to FTI.

Additionally, the proposal would require any FTI to which BEA and BLS would have access, either directly from IRS, from Census, or from each other, to be used for statistical purposes consistently with the Confidential Information Protection and Statistical Efficiency Act (CIPSEA). The three statistical agencies and state agencies would be subject to taxpayer privacy law, safeguards and penalties. They would also be subject to CIPSEA confidentiality safeguard procedures, requirements, and penalties. Conforming amendments to applicable statutes would be made as necessary to apply the taxpayer privacy law, including safeguards and penalties to BLS as well as Census and BEA. BLS would be required to monitor compliance by state agencies with the prescribed safeguard protocols.

The proposal would be effective upon enactment.

ELIMINATE CERTAIN REVIEWS CONDUCTED BY THE U.S. TREASURY INSPECTOR GENERAL FOR TAX ADMINISTRATION (TIGTA)

Current Law

Section 7803(d) requires the TIGTA to conduct reviews of certain administrative and civil actions and reviews of Internal Revenue Service (IRS) compliance with respect to certain requirements in order to comply with TIGTA's reporting requirements.

Reasons for Change

The statutory reviews that are proposed to be eliminated are of relatively low value and yield little in the way of performance measures. In order to make more efficient use of TIGTA's resources, TIGTA would prefer to redirect the resources applied to conduct these reviews to conducting high-risk audits.

Proposal

As requested by TIGTA, the proposal would eliminate TIGTA's obligation to report information regarding any administrative or civil actions related to Fair Tax Collection Practices violations in one of TIGTA's Semiannual Reports, review and certify annually that the IRS is complying with the requirements of section 6103(e)(8) regarding information on joint filers, and annually report on the IRS's compliance with sections 7521(b)(2) and (c) requiring IRS employees to stop a taxpayer interview whenever a taxpayer requests to consult with a representative and to obtain their immediate supervisor's approval to contact the taxpayer instead of the representative if the representative has unreasonably delayed the completion of an examination or investigation.

The proposal would revise the annual reporting requirement for all remaining provisions in the IRS Restructuring and Reform Act of 1998 to a biennial reporting requirement.

The proposal would be effective after December 31, 2011.

MODIFY INDEXING TO PREVENT DEFLATIONARY ADJUSTMENTS

Current Law

Many parameters of the tax system – including the size of personal exemptions and standard deductions, the width of income tax rate brackets, the amount of other deductions and credits, and the maximum amount of various saving and retirement deductions – may be adjusted annually for the effects of inflation. The adjustments are based on annual changes in the level of the Consumer Price Index (CPI-U). Depending on the particular tax parameter, the adjustment may be based on CPI-U for a particular month, its average for a calendar quarter, or its average for a 12-month period (with various ending dates). The adjusted values are rounded differently, as specified in the Internal Revenue Code.

When inflation adjustment of tax parameters was enacted, it was generally contemplated that indexing would result in upward adjustments to reflect inflation. If price levels decline for the year, the inflation adjustment provisions for most adjusted tax parameters permit the tax parameters to become smaller, so long as they do not decline to less than their base period values specified in the Code. However, the statutory provisions for the indexing of those tax parameters adjusted pursuant to section 415(d) (generally relating to benefits and contributions under qualified plans) are held at their previous year's level if the relevant price index declines. In subsequent years, they increase only to the extent that the relevant price index exceeds its highest preceding relevant level.

Reasons for Change

Between 2008 and 2009, for the first time since inflation adjustments were enacted, the annual index values used for two of the indexing methods declined for the relevant annual period. The index level relevant for section 415(d) adjustments fell, but by statute those parameters remain at their 2009 levels for 2010. (They did not increase for 2011.) Also, the maximum size of a cash method debt instrument, as adjusted under section 1274A(d)(2) decreased for 2010. Other tax parameters did not decrease, since the price index relevant for their adjustments did not decline between 2008 and 2009.

The 2008 to 2009 price index changes demonstrate that a year-to-year decrease is possible. Preventing tax parameters from falling if the underlying price levels fall would make the tax system a more effective automatic economic stabilizer than it is under current law. Holding tax parameters constant would also prevent reductions in certain tax benefits for saving and retirement which should not be affected by short-term price level reductions.

Proposal

The proposal would modify inflation adjustment provisions so as to prevent tax parameters from declining from the previous year's levels if the underlying price index falls. Future inflation-related increases would be based on the highest previous level of the price index relevant for adjusting the particular tax parameter.

The proposal would be effective beginning on the date of enactment.

PROGRAM INTEGRITY INITIATIVES

INCREASE LEVY AUTHORITY FOR PAYMENTS TO FEDERAL CONTRACTORS WITH DELINQUENT TAX DEBT

Current Law

If a federal vendor has an unpaid tax liability, the Internal Revenue Service (IRS) can levy 100 percent of any payment due to the vendor for goods or services sold or leased to the federal government.

Reason for Change

The statutory language "goods or services sold or leased" has been interpreted as excluding payments for the sale or lease of real estate or other types of property not considered "goods or services."

Proposal

The proposal would amend the statute to clarify that the IRS can levy 100 percent of any payment due to a federal vendor with unpaid tax liabilities, including payments made for the sale or lease of real estate and other types of property not considered "goods or services."

The proposal would be effective for payments made after the date of enactment.

INCREASE LEVY AUTHORITY FOR PAYMENTS TO MEDICARE PROVIDERS WITH DELINQUENT TAX DEBT

Current Law

Under the Medicare Improvement for Patients and Providers Act of 2008, the Treasury Department is authorized to continuously levy up to 15 percent of a payment to a Medicare provider in order to collect delinquent tax debt. Through the Federal Payment Levy Program, Treasury deducts (levies) a portion of a Government payment to an individual or business in order to collect unpaid taxes.

Reasons for Change

Certain Medicare providers fail to comply with their Federal income tax and/or employment tax obligations. Expanding to 100 percent the amount of Federal payments that can be levied for such providers will help recover a greater amount of delinquent taxes and will promote these providers' compliance with their Federal tax obligations.

Proposal

The proposal would allow Treasury to levy up to 100 percent of a payment to a Medicare provider to collect unpaid taxes.

The proposal would be effective for payments made after the date of enactment.

MODIFIED PAY-AS-YOU-GO (PAYGO) BASELINE

An important step in addressing the nation's fiscal problems is to be upfront about them, and to establish a revenue baseline that accurately measures where we are before new policies are enacted. This Budget does so by adjusting the Budget Enforcement Act (BEA) baseline to reflect the cost of the current policy path, to the extent current policy can be determined. The BEA baseline, which is commonly used in budgeting, reflects the projected receipts level under current law, with very limited exceptions. But it is widely believed that a number of future tax law changes scheduled under current law are unlikely to occur. These scheduled, but unlikely to occur, changes include the expiration of many of the tax cuts enacted by the Economic Growth and Tax Relief Reconciliation Act of 2001 (EGTRRA) and the Job Growth and Tax Relief Reconciliation Act of 2003 (JGTRRA), and extended by the Tax Relief, Unemployment Insurance Reauthorization, and Job Creation Act of 2010 (TRUIRJCA). Therefore current law does not provide a reasonable benchmark for judging the effect of new legislation.

Congress recognized that the expiration of a number of tax provisions was unrealistic, and allowed certain adjustments to the cost of legislation in the Statutory Pay-As-You-Go (PAYGO) Act of 2010 (Public Law 111-139). The Statutory PAYGO Act requires that new legislation changing taxes, fees, or mandatory expenditures, taken together, must not increase projected deficits. It establishes four cases for which an adjustment to the cost of legislation may be made, effectively exempting Congress from requiring tax or spending offsets to pay for these provisions if they are enacted by December 31, 2011. The excepted tax provisions relate to the Estate and Gift Tax, the Alternative Minimum Tax (AMT) and most provisions of EGTRRA and JGTRRA.[11]

Many of the excepted tax provisions were adopted on a temporary basis (usually through tax year 2012) by TRUIRJCA.

As a result, the Administration views adoption of the PAYGO adjustments as the appropriate baseline for considering further tax policy changes after TRUIRJCA expires, with two modifications to the Estate and Gift and AMT provisions. Specifically, the Statutory PAYGO Act adjustments to cost estimates and modifications for the Administration's baseline include:

Estate and Gift Tax – the Administration's baseline assumes that the Estate and Gift Tax provisions in effect for tax year 2009 are permanently extended, once Public Law 111-312 expires. This provides for an exemption of $3.5 million per estate (not indexed) and a tax rate of 45 percent, for decedents dying after December 31, 2012. Under current law, the Estate and Gift Tax provisions are set to revert to the levels provided under pre-2001 law (which include a lower exemption and higher rates than in effect in 2009). The Statutory PAYGO Act allows an adjustment for the extension of 2009 parameters only through December 31, 2011; however, since Congress recently enacted more generous estate tax provisions through 2012, there is

---

[11]Statutory PAYGO also provides for an adjustment for the cost of Medicare payments to physicians that are in excess of what payments would be under the sustainable growth rate formula. Congress has, however, recently chosen to pay for these Medicare expenditures. Similarly, the Administration's baseline does not except these Medicare payments, effectively assuming that continuation of payments in excess of the sustainable growth rate formula should be paid for.

considerable expectation that future legislation will provide more generous treatment than pre-2001 law.

AMT – the Administration's baseline assumes that the 2011 AMT parameters are permanently indexed for inflation after 2011. The baseline also allows non-refundable credits to be claimed against the AMT. The Statutory PAYGO Act allows an adjustment for the cost of extending AMT relief through December 31, 2011 only; however, Congress has repeatedly extended AMT relief and it is reasonable to expect similar legislation in the future.

Middle-class tax cuts – the Statutory PAYGO Act allows an adjustment for the permanent extension of the "middle-class tax cuts" in effect for tax year 2010, as provided under EGTRRA and JGTRRA and any amendments through December 31, 2009. Specifically, the PAYGO exceptions and the Administration's baseline include the cost of permanently extending:

- The 10-percent income tax bracket and the reduction of the 28 and 31-percent tax rates to 25 and 28 percent as provided under section 101(a) of EGTRRA.

- The reduction of the 36 percent tax rate to 33 percent as provided for under section 101(a) of EGTRRA, but only for taxpayers with adjusted gross income (AGI) of $200,000 or less for single filers or $250,000 or less for married filers (in 2009 dollars, indexed for inflation thereafter). The modified PAYGO baseline does not allow extension of the EGTRRA/JGTRRA tax rate cuts for upper-income families. Instead, these rate cuts would expire, and the top ordinary income tax rate would be 39.6 percent beginning in 2013.

- The child tax credit as provided under section 201 of EGTRRA and amended by the American Recovery and Reinvestment Act of 2009 (Public Law 111-5, or ARRA); that is, a credit of $1,000 per child, allowed against regular tax and the AMT, and refundable up to an amount equal to 15 percent of earned income in excess of $3,000 (not indexed).

- Tax benefits for married couples as provided for under title III of EGTRRA and amended by ARRA; that is, the increase in the standard deduction for joint filers to equal twice that of single taxpayers, the expansion of the 15-percent tax bracket for joint filers to twice the width of that for single taxpayers, and the $5,000 increase in the starting point of the earned income tax credit (EITC) phase-out range for joint filers (indexed beginning in 2010). Title III of EGTRRA and the baseline also include several modifications to simplify and improve compliance with the EITC.

- The expanded adoption tax credit as provided for under section 202 of EGTRRA; that is, a maximum credit of $10,000 (indexed for inflation after 2002) for adoptions of children with special-needs (without regard to expenses) and expenses related to other adoptions, allowed against regular tax and the AMT.

- The dependent care tax credit as provided for under section 204 of EGTRRA; that is, the maximum credit is $1,050 for one qualifying individual and $2,100 for two qualifying individuals.

- The employer-provided child care tax credit as provided for under section 205 of EGTRRA.

- The education tax benefits as provided for under title IV of EGTRRA. These benefits include an exclusion of up to $5,250 in employer provided education assistance; an increase in the phase-out range and elimination of the 60-month limit on the deductibility of student loan interest payments; and an exclusion from income of awards received under certain health professional programs.

- The reduction in tax rates on capital gains from 10 and 20 percent to 0 and 15 percent and the taxation of dividends at capital gains rather than ordinary rates, as provided for under sections 301 and 302 of JGTRRA, but only for taxpayers with AGI of $200,000 or less for single filers or $250,000 or less for married filers (in 2009 dollars, indexed for inflation thereafter).

- The elimination of the phase-out of personal exemptions and the elimination of the limitation on itemized deductions (Pease), as provided for under sections 102 and 103 of EGTRRA, but only for taxpayers with AGI of $200,000 or less for single filers or $250,000 or less for married filers (in 2009 dollars, indexed for inflation thereafter).

- The increased limits on expensing small business assets under section 179(b) of the Internal Revenue Code as provided for under section 202 of JGTRRA; that is, businesses would be able to expense up to $125,000 of investment, phased out dollar for dollar after investment reaches $500,000 (dollar levels indexed for inflation from 2006).

The Administration interprets sections 7(a)(4)(D) and 7(f)(1)(I)-(K), of the Statutory PAYGO Act as follows: (1) In applying the AGI thresholds of $200,000 for single filers and $250,000 for joint filers we assume that the threshold for married filing separately taxpayers is set equal to half that of married filing jointly taxpayers, the AGI threshold for head of household filers is set half-way between that of single and married filing jointly taxpayers at $225,000, and the AGI threshold for qualifying widows and widowers is set equal to that for married filing jointly taxpayers; (2) All taxpayers face the same income tax rate schedule for their applicable filing status; that is, high-income taxpayers benefit from lower rates exempted under the Statutory PAYGO Act; (3) The amount of taxable income at which the marginal tax rate increases from 33 percent to 36 percent is equal to the applicable AGI threshold less the standard deduction for the taxpayer's filing status and one personal exemption (two in the case of married filing jointly taxpayers); and (4) The AGI thresholds are indexed for inflation after 2009.

For 2011 the Administration's baseline is current law (including extension of the EGTRRA/JGTRRA tax cuts for upper-income families) and for 2012 it is current law (including extension of the EGTRRA/ JGTRRA tax cuts for upper-income families) with AMT relief as described above.

TABLES OF REVENUE ESTIMATES

Revenue estimates begin on next page.

Table 1: Revenue Estimates of FY 2012 Budget Proposals 1/ 2/ 3/

Fiscal Years
(in millions of dollars)

	2011	2012	2013	2014	2015	2016	2017	2018	2019	2020	2021	2012-2016	2012-2021
Tax cuts for families and individuals													
Provide $250 refundable tax credit for Federal, State and local government retirees not eligible for social security 4/	-216	-159	0	0	0	0	0	0	0	0	0	-159	-159
Extend the earned income tax credit (EITC) for larger families 4/	0	0	-81	-1,422	-1,442	-1,469	-1,509	-1,544	-1,579	-1,610	-1,657	-4,414	-12,313
Expand the child and dependent care tax credit 4/	0	-283	-1,043	-1,045	-1,042	-1,039	-1,035	-1,036	-1,033	-1,028	-1,021	-4,452	-9,605
Provide for automatic enrollment in RAs and double the tax credit for small employer plan startup costs 4/	0	0	-638	-1,043	-1,100	-1,240	-1,448	-1,704	-2,015	-2,381	-2,809	-4,021	-14,378
Extend the American opportunity tax credit (AOTC) 4/	0	0	-650	-10,772	-10,832	-11,552	-11,533	-11,364	-12,111	-12,117	-12,665	-33,806	-93,596
Provide exclusion from income for certain student loan forgiveness					*Negligible Revenue Effect*								
Tax qualified dividends and net long-term capital gains at a 20-percent rate for upper-income taxpayers	0	-7,868	-9,582	-5,405	-9,416	-12,964	-14,688	-15,119	-15,586	-16,158	-16,885	-45,235	-123,671
Subtotal, tax cuts for families and individuals	**-216**	**-8,310**	**-11,994**	**-19,687**	**-23,832**	**-28,264**	**-30,213**	**-30,767**	**-32,324**	**-33,294**	**-35,037**	**-92,087**	**-253,722**
Tax cuts for businesses													
Eliminate capital gains taxation on investments in small business stock	0	0	0	0	0	0	-183	-566	-1,055	-1,587	-2,026	0	-5,417
Enhance and make permanent the research and experimentation (R&E) tax credit	0	-4,510	-8,063	-8,884	-9,708	-10,520	-11,318	-12,103	-12,887	-13,686	-14,499	-41,785	-106,278
Provide additional tax credits for investment in qualified property used in a qualifying advanced energy manufacturing project ("48C")	0	-284	-731	-1,089	-1,138	-578	-120	73	115	64	27	-3,820	-3,661
Provide tax credit for energy-efficient commercial building property expenditures in place of existing tax deduction	0	-450	-425	-100	-25	-25	0	0	0	0	0	-1,025	-1,025
Subtotal, tax cuts for businesses	**0**	**-5,444**	**-9,219**	**-10,073**	**-10,871**	**-11,123**	**-11,621**	**-12,596**	**-13,827**	**-15,209**	**-16,498**	**-46,630**	**-116,381**
Incentives to promote regional growth													
Extend and modify the New Markets tax credit (NMTC)	-41	-62	-116	-183	-234	-263	-272	-264	-243	-170	-63	-858	-1,870
Reform and extend Build America bonds 4/	-1	-2	-2	-2	-4	-3	-3	-3	-3	-3	-3	-13	-28
Low-income housing tax credit (LIHTC) provisions:	-1	-5	-16	-32	-52	-71	-94	-116	-139	-162	-185	-176	-872
Encourage mixed-income occupancy by allowing LIHTC-supported projects to elect an average-income criterion	0	-1	-2	-3	-6	-8	-12	-15	-18	-21	-24	-20	-110
Provide 30-percent basis "boost" to properties that receive tax-exempt bond financing	-1	-4	-14	-29	-46	-63	-82	-101	-121	-141	-161	-156	-762
subtotal, LIHTC provisions	-1	-5	-16	-32	-52	-71	-94	-116	-139	-162	-185	-176	-872
Designate Growth Zones 4/	0	-279	-863	-860	-839	-815	-186	383	374	329	273	-3,656	-2,483
Restructure assistance to New York City: Provide tax incentives for transportation infrastructure	0	-200	-200	-200	-200	-200	-200	-200	-200	-200	-200	-1,000	-2,000
Subtotal, incentives to promote regional growth	**-43**	**-548**	**-1,197**	**-1,277**	**-1,329**	**-1,352**	**-755**	**-200**	**-211**	**-206**	**-178**	**-5,703**	**-7,263**
Continue certain expiring provisions through calendar year 2012 4/ 5/	**-282**	**-9,061**	**-10,182**	**-734**	**-372**	**-168**	**-61**	**-95**	**-122**	**-169**	**-192**	**-20,507**	**-21,146**
Other revenue changes and loophole closers													
Reform treatment of financial institutions and products:													
Impose a financial crisis responsibility fee	0	0	1,000	3,000	3,000	3,000	4,000	4,000	4,000	4,000	4,000	10,000	30,000
Require accrual of income on forward sale of corporate stock	1	5	12	19	26	33	36	38	40	42	44	96	296
Require ordinary treatment of income from day-to-day dealer activities for certain dealers of equity options and commodities	35	144	226	240	254	270	286	303	321	341	361	1,134	2,746
Modify the definition of "control" for purposes of section 249 of the Internal Revenue Code	0	9	15	16	17	17	18	19	20	21	22	74	174
subtotal, reform treatment of financial institutions and products	36	155	1,253	3,275	3,297	3,320	4,340	4,360	4,381	4,404	4,427	11,304	33,216
Reinstate Superfund taxes:													
Reinstate Superfund excise taxes	0	588	790	805	819	833	845	853	865	877	887	3,835	8,162
Reinstate Superfund environmental income tax	0	786	1,136	1,233	1,274	1,311	1,340	1,359	1,381	1,395	1,442	5,740	12,657
subtotal, reinstate Superfund taxes	0	1,374	1,926	2,038	2,093	2,144	2,185	2,212	2,246	2,272	2,329	9,575	20,819
Reform U.S. international tax system:													
Defer deduction of interest expense related to deferred income	0	2,986	5,138	5,396	5,636	5,861	6,080	3,114	1,103	1,149	1,202	25,017	37,665
Determine the foreign tax credit on a pooling basis	0	2,655	4,568	4,798	5,011	5,211	5,406	5,601	5,810	6,051	6,333	22,243	51,444
Tax currently excess returns associated with transfers of intangibles offshore	0	1,204	2,038	2,114	2,212	2,280	2,290	2,231	2,158	2,138	2,166	9,848	20,831
Limit shifting of income through intangible property transfers	0	29	63	90	118	148	178	209	242	276	315	448	1,668
Disallow the deduction for non-taxed reinsurance premiums paid to affiliates	0	129	223	237	250	264	277	289	302	315	328	1,103	2,614
Limit earnings stripping by expatriated entities	0	212	364	382	401	421	442	464	487	512	537	1,780	4,222
Modify the tax rules for dual capacity taxpayers	0	532	918	974	1,031	1,085	1,138	1,190	1,242	1,296	1,352	4,540	10,758
subtotal, reform U.S. international tax system	0	7,747	13,312	13,991	14,659	15,270	15,811	13,098	11,344	11,737	12,233	64,979	129,202
Reform treatment of insurance companies and products:													
Modify rules that apply to sales of life insurance contracts	0	8	42	82	97	115	134	154	177	203	231	344	1,243
Modify dividends-received deduction (DRD) for life insurance company separate accounts	0	172	465	547	579	605	607	585	555	528	503	2,368	5,146
Expand pro rata interest expense disallowance for corporate-owed life insurance	0	21	71	181	273	433	652	900	1,280	1,714	2,166	979	7,691
subtotal, reform treatment of insurance companies and products	0	201	578	810	949	1,153	1,393	1,639	2,012	2,445	2,900	3,691	14,080

	2011	2012	2013	2014	2015	2016	2017	2018	2019	2020	2021	2012-2016	2012-2021
Miscellaneous changes:													
Increase the Oil Spill Liability Trust Fund financing rate by one cent	0	35	46	46	46	46	46	46	47	46	47	219	451
Make unemployment insurance surtax permanent	0	1,375	1,413	1,449	1,477	1,503	1,526	1,543	1,558	1,577	1,594	7,217	15,015
Provide short-term tax relief to employers and expand Federal Unemployment Tax Act (FUTA) base	0	-1,714	-3,541	7,477	12,863	10,544	11,814	8,555	-34	-263	167	25,629	45,868
Repeal last-in, first-out (LIFO) method of accounting for inventories	0	0	2,598	5,649	6,484	6,457	6,435	6,387	6,337	6,293	6,240	21,188	52,880
Repeal gain limitation for dividends received in reorganization exchanges	0	47	79	81	84	86	89	92	94	97	100	377	849
Tax carried (profits) interests in investment partnerships as ordinary income	318	2,274	2,123	2,154	1,927	1,608	1,322	1,089	908	762	640	10,086	14,807
Deny deduction for punitive damages	0	0	23	34	35	35	36	36	37	37	39	127	312
Repeal lower-of-cost-or-market (LCM) inventory accounting method	0	0	188	1,435	2,334	1,532	1,358	309	323	337	352	5,489	8,168
subtotal, *miscellaneous changes*	318	2,017	2,929	18,325	25,250	21,811	22,626	18,057	9,270	8,886	9,179	70,332	138,350
Subtotal, other revenue changes and loophole closers	354	11,498	19,998	38,439	46,248	43,698	46,365	39,366	29,253	29,744	31,068	169,881	335,667
Eliminate fossil-fuel preferences													
Eliminate oil and gas preferences:													
Repeal enhanced oil recovery (EOR) credit 6/	0	0	0	0	0	0	0	0	0	0	0	0	0
Repeal credit for oil and gas produced from marginal wells 6/	0	0	0	0	0	0	0	0	0	0	0	0	0
Repeal expensing of intangible drilling costs (IDCs)	0	1,875	2,512	1,762	1,403	1,331	1,124	830	640	523	447	8,883	12,447
Repeal deduction for tertiary injectants	0	6	10	10	10	10	10	9	9	9	9	46	92
Repeal exception to passive loss limitation for working interests in oil and natural gas properties	0	23	27	24	22	21	19	18	17	16	16	117	203
Repeal percentage depletion for oil and natural gas wells	0	607	1,038	1,079	1,111	1,142	1,177	1,211	1,243	1,273	1,321	4,977	11,202
Repeal domestic manufacturing deduction for oil and natural gas companies	0	902	1,558	1,653	1,749	1,842	1,932	2,020	2,108	2,200	2,296	7,704	18,260
Increase geological and geophysical amortization period for independent producers to seven years	0	59	215	330	306	230	152	75	22	9	10	1,140	1,408
subtotal, *eliminate oil and gas preferences*	0	3,472	5,360	4,858	4,601	4,576	4,414	4,163	4,039	4,030	4,099	22,867	43,672
Eliminate coal preferences:													
Repeal expensing of exploration and development costs	0	27	45	47	49	51	50	48	47	45	38	219	447
Repeal percentage depletion for hard mineral fossil fuels	0	78	129	129	130	135	139	145	149	154	165	601	1,353
Repeal capital gains treatment for royalties	0	11	13	22	31	38	43	47	51	55	58	115	369
Repeal domestic manufacturing deduction for coal and other hard mineral fossil fuels	0	20	35	38	39	41	44	45	48	49	51	173	410
subtotal, *eliminate coal preferences*	0	136	222	236	249	265	276	285	295	303	312	1,108	2,579
Subtotal, eliminate fossil-fuel preferences	6	3,608	5,682	5,094	4,850	4,841	4,690	4,448	4,334	4,333	4,411	23,975	46,191
Simplify the tax code													
Allow vehicle seller to claim qualified plug-in electric-drive motor vehicle credit	0	-64	-30	-59	-53	135	166	-232	-103	-11	-18	-71	-269
Eliminate minimum required distribution (MRD) rules for IRA/plan balances of $50,000 or less	0	-2	-5	-7	-9	-12	-15	-19	-23	-28	-31	-35	-151
Allow all inherited plan and RA balances to be rolled over within 60 days								*Negligible Revenue Effect*					
Clarify exception to recapture of unrecognized gain on sale of stock to an employee stock ownership plan (ESOP)							*Negligible Revenue Effect*						
Repeal non-qualified preferred stock (NQPS) designation	22	101	112	110	105	97	87	77	68	61	54	525	872
Revise and simplify the "fractions rule"	-5	-19	-22	-24	-23	-24	-24	-26	-26	-26	-28	-112	-242
Reform preferential dividend rule for publicly traded real estate investment trusts (REITs)								*Negligible Revenue Effect*					
Reform excise tax based on investment income of private foundations	-1	-4	-4	-5	-5	-5	-6	-6	-6	-7	-7	-23	-55
Simplify tax-exempt bonds:													
Simplify arbitrage investment restrictions	0	-4	-13	-21	-30	-40	-49	-59	-68	-76	-86	-108	-446
Simplify single-family housing mortgage bond targeting requirements	0	0	0	-1	-1	-1	-1	-3	-3	-3	-3	-3	-16
Streamline private business limits on governmental bonds	0	-1	-3	-5	-7	-9	-11	-13	-15	-17	-19	-25	-100
subtotal, *simplify tax exempt bonds*	0	-5	-16	-27	-38	-50	-61	-75	-86	-96	-108	-136	-562
Subtotal, simplify the tax code	16	7	35	-12	-23	141	147	-281	-176	-107	-138	148	-407
Reduce the tax gap and make reforms													
Expand Information Reporting:													
Repeal and modify information reporting on payments to corporations and payments for property	0	-475	-618	-756	-929	-961	-1,000	-1,047	-1,096	-1,147	-1,180	-3,739	-9,209
Require information reporting for private separate accounts of life insurance companies	0	0	1	2	3	3	4	5	6	7	8	9	39
Require a certified Taxpayer Identification Number (T N) from contractors and allow certain withholding	21	48	81	110	115	121	126	132	138	144	150	475	1,165
subtotal, *expand information reporting*	21	-427	-536	-644	-811	-837	-870	-910	-952	-996	-1,022	-3,255	-8,005
Improve compliance by businesses:													
Require greater electronic filing of returns							*No Revenue Effect*						
Authorize the Department of the Treasury to require additional information to be included in electronically filed Form 5500 Annual Reports							*No Revenue Effect*						
Implement standards clarifying when employee leasing companies can be held liable for their clients' Federal employment taxes	0	4	5	6	6	6	7	7	7	8	8	27	64

Fiscal Years

(in millions of dollars)

	2011	2012	2013	2014	2015	2016	2017	2018	2019	2020	2021	2012-2016	2012-2021
Increase certainty with respect to worker classification	0	12	230	1,237	956	819	904	994	1,088	1,186	1,284	3,254	8,710
Repeal special estimated tax payment provision for certain insurance companies						*Negligible Revenue Effect*							
Eliminate special rules modifying the amount of estimated tax payments by corporations	0	0	0	-53,610	4,320	49,290	0	0	-5,630	5,630	0	0	0
subtotal, improve compliance by businesses	0	16	235	-52,367	5,282	50,115	911	1,001	-4,535	6,824	1,292	3,281	8,774
Strengthen tax administration:													
Revise offer-in-compromise application rules	0	2	2	2	2	2	3	3	3	3	3	10	25
Expand RS access to information in the National Directory of New Hires for tax administration purposes						*No Revenue Effect*							
Make repeated willful failure to file a tax return a felony	0	0	0	0	1	1	1	1	2	2	2	2	10
Facilitate tax compliance with local jurisdictions	0	0	0	0	1	1	1	1	1	1	1	2	7
Extend of statute of limitations where State adjustment affects Federal tax liability	0	0	0	0	2	4	4	4	4	4	5	6	27
Improve investigative disclosure statute	0	0	0	0	1	1	1	1	2	2	2	2	10
Require taxpayers who prepare their returns electronically but file their returns on paper to print their returns with a 2-D bar code						*No Revenue Effect*							
Require prisons located in the U.S. to provide information to the RS	0	10	15	16	16	17	18	18	18	19	19	74	166
Allow the RS to absorb credit and debit card processing fees for certain tax payments	0	1	1	2	2	2	2	2	2	2	2	8	18
subtotal, strengthen tax administration	0	13	18	20	25	28	30	30	32	33	34	104	263
Expand penalties:													
Impose a penalty on failure to comply with electronic filing requirements	0	0	0	0	0	1	1	1	2	2	2	1	9
Increase penalty imposed on paid preparers who fail to comply with EITC due diligence requirements	0	13	27	31	32	34	35	35	36	37	38	137	318
subtotal, expand penalties	0	13	27	31	32	35	36	36	38	39	40	138	327
Subtotal, reduce the tax gap and make reforms	21	-335	-256	-52,960	4,628	49,341	107	157	-5,417	5,900	344	268	1,359
Modify estate and gift tax valuation discounts and make other reforms													
Make permanent the portability of unused exemption between spouses	0	0	0	-107	-217	-321	-421	-516	-609	-699	-791	-645	-3,681
Require consistency in value for transfer and income tax purposes	0	127	171	182	192	204	216	229	243	258	273	876	2,095
Modify rules on valuation discounts	0	806	860	1,558	1,687	1,823	1,966	2,116	2,277	2,444	2,629	6,734	18,166
Require a minimum term for grantor retained annuity trusts (GRATs)	0	-5	46	93	160	231	308	389	477	570	670	545	2,959
Limit duration of generation-skipping transfer (GST) tax exemption						*Negligible Revenue Effect*							
Subtotal, estate and gift tax	0	948	1,077	1,726	1,822	1,937	2,069	2,218	2,388	2,573	2,781	7,510	19,539
Upper-income tax provision Reduce the value of certain tax expenditures	0	6,008	18,996	26,418	29,766	32,696	35,699	38,644	41,496	44,388	47,180	113,884	321,291
User fees Reform inland waterways funding	0	0	196	163	135	72	72	71	69	70	69	566	917
Other initiatives													
Allow offset of Federal income tax refunds to collect delinquent State income taxes for out-of-state residents						*No Revenue Effect*							
Authorize the limited sharing of business tax return information to improve the accuracy of important measures of our economy						*No Revenue Effect*							
Eliminate certain reviews conducted by the U.S. Treasury Inspector General for Tax Administration (TIGTA)						*No Revenue Effect*							
Modify indexing to prevent deflationary adjustments						*No Revenue Effect*							
Subtotal, other initiatives	0	0	0	0	0	0	0	0	0	0	0	0	0
Program integrity initiatives													
Increase levy authority for payments to Federal contractors with delinquent tax debt	5	59	61	64	67	69	73	76	80	83	87	320	719
Increase levy authority for payments to Medicare providers with delinquent tax debt	17	64	68	71	74	76	76	78	80	80	81	353	748
Subtotal, program integrity initiatives	22	123	129	135	141	145	149	154	160	163	168	673	1,467
Total Effect of FY 2012 Budget Tax Proposals Relative to the Adjusted Baseline	-122	-1,466	13,165	-12,768	51,063	91,974	46,638	41,119	25,623	38,186	33,978	141,978	327,622
Total receipt effect	15	-294	16,028	-3,245	61,772	103,950	59,729	55,414	41,484	55,332	52,701	178,211	442,871
Total outlay effect	137	1,162	2,863	9,523	10,709	11,976	13,091	14,295	15,861	17,146	18,723	36,233	115,349

Department of the Treasury

Notes:

1/ Presentation in this table does not reflect the order in which these proposals were estimated.

2/ Table 2 below details the budgetary impact of adjusting the Budget Enforcement Act baseline to extend certain tax policies. These extensions were were estimated before the policy proposals shown in this table.

3/ Tables 15-3 and 15-4 in the Analytical Perspectives of the FY 2012 Budget includes the effects of a number of proposals that are not reflected here. These proposals would levy a fee on the production of hardrock minerals to restore abandoned mines, expand short-time compensation unemployment program, increase fees for Migratory Bird Hunting and Conservation Stamps, support certain trade initiatives, reauthorize surface transportation, enhance UI integrity, and implement program integrity allocation adjustments for the IRS.

4/ This provision affects both receipts and outlays. The combined effects are shown here and the outlays effects included in these estimates are detailed in Table 3.

5/ Detail on the estimates included in this item are reported in Table 4.

6/ This provision is estimated to have zero receipt effect under the Administration's current projections for energy prices.

Table 2: Adjustments to the Budget Enforcement Act Baseline for the Adjusted Baseline 1/

| | | | | | Fiscal Years | | | | | | | | |
| | | | | | (in millions of dollars) | | | | | | | | |
	2011	2012	2013	2014	2015	2016	2017	2018	2019	2020	2021	2012-2016	2012-2021
Adjustments to BEA baseline													
Continue the 2001 and 2003 tax cuts for middle-income taxpayers:													
Tax dividends with a 0%/15% rate structure for taxpayers with income below $250,000 (joint) and $200,000 (single)	0	0	-4,170	-9,047	-10,471	-11,804	-12,589	-12,865	-13,083	-13,326	-13,627	-35,492	-100,982
Tax capital gains with a 0%/15% rate structure for taxpayers with income below $250,000 (joint) and $200,000 (single)		-757	-1,949	-2,754	-3,837	-5,231	-6,086	-6,389	-6,616	-6,800	-6,965	-14,528	-47,384
Expand expensing for small businesses		0	-5,632	-8,133	-6,413	-5,225	-4,364	-3,834	-3,603	-3,526	-3,561	-25,403	-44,291
Reduce marginal individual income tax rates		0	-44,118	-62,378	-63,023	-63,417	-64,279	-64,832	-65,241	-65,522	-65,566	-232,936	-558,376
Repeal the personal exemption phaseout (PEP)		0	-10	-21	-23	-24	-27	-29	-32	-34	-34	-78	-234
Repeal the limitation on itemized deductions (Pease)		0	-479	-1,035	-1,165	-1,272	-1,380	-1,484	-1,585	-1,685	-1,790	-3,951	-11,875
Increase the child credit 2/		0	-6,326	-44,395	-44,803	-45,120	-45,454	-45,697	-46,081	-46,363	-46,687	-140,644	-370,926
Provide relief for married taxpayers 2/		0	-5,479	-11,619	-11,503	-11,223	-11,076	-10,850	-10,635	-10,501	-10,512	-39,824	-93,398
Provide education incentives		-4	-894	-1,843	-1,914	-1,987	-2,064	-2,145	-2,228	-2,316	-2,410	-6,642	-17,805
Provide other incentives for families and children		6	-114	-644	-624	-602	-584	-566	-544	-522	-520	-1,978	-4,714
Extend estate, gift, and generation-skipping transfer taxes at 2009 parameters	-1,258	-1,860	-4,841	-23,977	-26,449	-29,198	-31,704	-34,517	-36,858	-39,181	-41,625	-86,325	-270,210
Index to inflation the 2011 parameters of the AMT	0	-33,292	-106,436	-106,467	-123,773	-142,376	-162,269	-183,068	-206,156	-230,455	-255,894	-512,344	-1,550,186
Total Effect of Adjustments to BEA Baseline	**-1,258**	**-35,907**	**-180,448**	**-272,313**	**-293,998**	**-317,479**	**-341,876**	**-366,276**	**-392,662**	**-420,231**	**-449,191**	**-1,100,145**	**-3,070,381**
Total receipt effect	-1,258	-35,907	-179,056	-244,461	-266,131	-289,650	-313,942	-338,328	-364,554	-392,018	-420,731	-1,015,205	-2,844,778
Total outlay effect	0	0	1,392	27,852	27,867	27,829	27,934	27,948	28,108	28,213	28,460	84,940	225,603

Department of the Treasury

Notes:

1/ Proposals in this table were estimated before the proposals shown in Table 1.

2/ This provision affects both receipts and outlays. The combined effects are shown here and the outlays effects included in these estimates are detailed in Table 3 below.

Table 3: Outlay Effects Included in Revenue Estimates

| | | | | | Fiscal Years | | | | | | | | |
| | | | | | (in millions of dollars) | | | | | | | | |
	2011	2012	2013	2014	2015	2016	2017	2018	2019	2020	2021	2012-2016	2012-2021
Increase the child credit	0	0	1,187	23,753	23,812	23,807	23,903	23,908	24,030	24,112	24,300	72,559	192,812
Provide relief for married taxpayers	0	0	205	4,099	4,055	4,022	4,031	4,040	4,078	4,101	4,160	12,381	32,791
Provide $250 refundable credit for federal, state and local government retirees not eligible for social security		47										47	47
Extend the earned income tax credit (EITC) for larger families	0	0	69	1,372	1,384	1,404	1,436	1,463	1,490	1,512	1,551	4,229	11,681
Expand the child and dependent care tax credit	0	0	337	347	354	363	372	386	398	410	420	1,401	3,387
Provide for automatic enrollment in IRAs and double the tax credit for small employer plan startup costs	0	0	38	66	71	79	90	105	122	142	167	254	880
Extend American opportunity tax credit	0	0	16	4,465	4,425	4,655	4,608	4,531	4,791	4,775	5,038	13,561	37,304
Reform and extend Build America bonds	105	599	1,580	2,793	4,048	5,314	6,575	7,830	9,080	10,324	11,561	14,334	59,704
Designate Growth Zones	0	14	34	43	43	40	10	-20	-20	-17	-14	174	113
Continue certain expiring provisions through calendar year 2012:													
Grants for specified energy property in lieu of tax credits	0	357	426	428	383	121	0	0	0	0	0	1,715	1,715
Temporary increase in limit on cover over of rum excise tax revenues (from $10.50 to $13.25 per proof gallon) to Puerto Rico and the Virgin Islands	0	80	26	0	0	0	0	0	0	0	0	106	106
Expansion of the adoption credit	0	0	300	0	0	0	0	0	0	0	0	300	300
Health coverage tax credit (HCTC)	32	65	37	9	1	0	0	0	0	0	0	112	112
Total Outlay Effect of Proposals	**137**	**1,162**	**4,255**	**37,376**	**38,576**	**39,805**	**41,025**	**42,243**	**43,969**	**45,359**	**47,183**	**121,173**	**340,952**

Department of the Treasury

Table 4: Supplementary Detail on the Effects of Continuing Certain Expiring Provisions Through Calendar Year 2012 1/

						Fiscal Years (in millions of dollars)						
	2011	2012	2013	2014	2015	2016	2017	2018	2019	2020	2021	2012-2016	2012-2021
Continue certain expiring provisions through calendar year 2012													
Energy:													
Incentives for biodiesel and renewable diesel	0	-465	-462	-3	-2	-1	-1	0	0	0	0	-933	-934
Credit for construction of energy efficient new homes	0	-34	-33	-10	-8	-5	-4	-2	-2	-2	-1	-90	-101
Incentives for alternative fuel and alternative fuel mixtures	0	-34	-168	0	0	0	0	0	0	0	0	-202	-202
Special rule to implement electric transmission restructuring	-3	-205	-118	43	52	52	52	52	54	22	0	-176	4
Grants for specified energy property in lieu of tax credits 2/	0	-188	-204	-119	-74	3	34	29	26	23	24	-582	-446
Incentives for alcohol fuels	0	-2,346	-2,430	-8	-3	-2	-2	0	0	0	0	-4,789	-4,791
Extension and modification of section 25C nonbusiness energy property	0	-478	-585	0	0	0	0	-1	0	0	0	-1,063	-1,063
Credit for energy efficient appliances	0	-7	-6	-5	-3	-2	-1	-1	0	0	0	-23	-25
Alternative fuel vehicle refueling property (non-hydrogen refueling property)	5	8	5	2	1	0	0	0	0	0	0	16	16
subtotal, energy	2	-3,749	-4,001	-100	-37	45	78	78	78	43	23	-7,842	-7,542
Individual tax relief:													
Above-the-line deduction of up to $250 for teacher classroom expenses	0	-19	-171	0	0	0	0	0	0	0	0	-190	-190
Deduction of State and local general sales taxes	0	-905	-1,357	0	0	0	0	0	0	0	0	-2,262	-2,262
Contributions of capital gain real property made for qualified conservation purposes	0	-6	-27	0	0	0	0	0	0	0	0	-33	-33
Deduction for qualified tuition and related expenses	0	-88	-791	0	0	0	0	0	0	0	0	-879	-879
Tax-free distributions from IRAs to certain public charities for individuals age 70 1/2 or older, not to exceed $100,000 per taxpayer per year	0	-226	-258	-46	-25	-21	-17	-14	-10	-5	-3	-576	-625
Estate tax look-through for certain RIC stock held by nonresidents	0	-2	-5	-1	0	0	0	0	0	0	0	-8	-8
Parity for exclusion for employer-provided mass transit and parking benefits	0	-33	-43	0	0	0	0	0	0	0	0	-76	-76
subtotal, individual tax relief	0	-1,279	-2,652	-47	-25	-21	-17	-14	-10	-5	-3	-4,024	-4,073
Business tax relief:													
Indian employment tax credit	0	-10	-18	-14	-11	-9	-6	-5	-5	-3	-3	-62	-84
50% tax credit for certain expenditures for maintaining railroad tracks	-123	-112	-34	-16	-9	-4	-2	-1	0	0	0	-175	-178
Mine rescue team training credit	0	-4	-2	0	0	0	0	0	0	0	0	-6	-6
Employer wage credit for activated military reservists	0	-1	-1	0	0	0	0	0	0	0	0	-2	-2
15-year straight line cost recovery for qualified leasehold, restaurant and retail improvements	0	-38	-108	-141	-143	-144	-144	-144	-145	-145	-145	-574	-1,297
7-year recovery period for certain motorsports racing track facilities	0	-6	-17	-17	-10	-4	-3	-4	-1	6	9	-54	-47
Accelerated depreciation for business property on Indian reservations	0	-160	-265	-82	36	83	99	54	17	-6	-13	-388	-237
Enhanced charitable deduction for contributions of food inventory	0	-12	-21	0	0	0	0	0	0	0	0	-33	-33
Enhanced charitable deduction for contributions of book inventories to public schools	0	-43	-77	0	0	0	0	0	0	0	0	-120	-120
Enhanced charitable deduction for corporate contributions of computer inventory for educational purposes	0	-102	-68	0	0	0	0	0	0	0	0	-170	-170
Election to expense mine safety equipment	0	-1	-1	0	0	0	0	0	0	0	0	-2	-2
Special expensing rules for certain film and television productions	-125	-187	-131	-92	-57	-25	-9	-1	0	0	0	-492	-502
Expensing of "Brownfields" environmental remediation costs	0	-210	-118	13	12	12	12	11	11	10	10	-291	-237
Deduction allowable with respect to income attributable to domestic production activities in Puerto Rico	0	-106	-70	0	0	0	0	0	0	0	0	-176	-176
Modify tax treatment of certain payments under existing arrangements to controlling exempt organizations	0	-8	-6	0	0	0	0	0	0	0	0	-14	-14
Treatment of certain dividends of regulated investment companies (RICs)	0	-8	-44	0	0	0	0	0	0	0	0	-52	-52
Extend the treatment of RICs as "qualified investment entities" under section 897	0	-10	-7	0	0	0	0	0	0	0	0	-17	-17
Exception under subpart F for active financing income	0	-1,850	-1,233	0	0	0	0	0	0	0	0	-3,083	-3,083
Look-through treatment of payments between related CFCs under foreign personal holding company income rules	0	-402	-268	0	0	0	0	0	0	0	0	-670	-670
Basis adjustment to stock of S corporations making charitable contributions of property	0	-8	-12	0	0	0	0	0	0	0	0	-20	-20
Tax incentives for investment in the District of Columbia	0	-13	-31	0	-3	-7	-16	-21	-16	-17	-17	-54	-141
Temporary increase in limit on cover over of rum excise tax revenues (from $10.50 to $13.25 per proof gallon) to Puerto Rico and the Virgin Islands 2/	0	-80	-26	0	0	0	0	0	0	0	0	-106	-106
Economic development credit for American Samoa	0	-6	-8	0	0	0	0	0	0	0	0	-14	-14
Work opportunity tax credit	0	-140	-276	-184	-83	-41	-7	0	0	0	0	-724	-731
Qualified zone academy bonds	0	0	0	0	0	0	0	0	0	0	0	0	0
Premiums for mortgage insurance deductible as interest that is qualified residence interest	-2	-102	-144	10	9	7	5	4	2	1	0	-220	-208
subtotal, business tax relief	-250	-3,619	-2,986	-523	-259	-132	-71	-107	-137	-154	-159	-7,519	-8,147

| | | | | | | | Fiscal Years | | | | | | |
| | | | | | | | (in millions of dollars) | | | | | | |
	2011	2012	2013	2014	2015	2016	2017	2018	2019	2020	2021	2012-2016	2012-2021
Temporary disaster provisions:													
New York Liberty Zone: tax exempt bond financing	0	-3	-12	-18	-18	-18	-18	-18	-18	-18	-18	-69	-159
GO Zone:													
Extend the higher credit rate for GO Zone rehabilitation	0	-13	-18	-6	0	0	0	0	0	0	0	-37	-37
Extend the placed-in-service deadline for GO Zone low-income housing credits	0	-1	-2	-4	-5	-4	-5	-5	-5	-5	-4	-16	-40
Tax-exempt bond financing	0	-7	-30	-30	-30	-30	-30	-30	-30	-30	-30	-127	-277
Bonus depreciation for specified GO Zone extension property	0	-100	-64	5	5	5	5	5	5	5	5	-149	-124
subtotal, temporary disaster relief	0	-124	-126	-53	-48	-47	-48	-48	-48	-48	-47	-398	-637
Other tax provisions:													
Expansion of the adoption credit 2/	0	-221	-374	0	0	0	0	0	0	0	0	-595	-595
Plug-in hybrid conversion credit	0	0	-3	0	0	0	0	0	0	0	0	-3	-3
L HTC treatment of military housing allowances	0	0	0	-1	-1	-2	-2	-3	-4	-4	-5	-4	-22
Green bonds	0	-1	-1	-1	-1	-1	-1	-1	-1	-1	-1	-5	-10
Health coverage tax credit (HCTC) 2/	-34	-68	-39	-9	-1	0	0	0	0	0	0	-117	-117
subtotal, other tax provisions	-34	-290	-417	-11	-3	-3	-3	-4	-5	-5	-6	-724	-747
Total Effect of Extending Expiring Provisions Through 2012	**-282**	**-9,061**	**-10,182**	**-734**	**-372**	**-168**	**-61**	**-95**	**-122**	**-169**	**-192**	**-20,507**	**-21,146**
Total receipt effect	-250	-8,559	-9,393	-297	12	-37	-61	-95	-122	-169	-192	-18,274	-18,913
Total outlay effect	32	502	789	437	384	121	0	0	0	0	0	2,233	2,233

Department of the Treasury

Notes:

1/ Trade provisions are excluded from this table; extending expiring trade provisions would reduce receipts by $584 million in 2011, $898 million in 2012, and $277 million in 2013.

2/ This provision affects both receipts and outlays. The combined effects are shown here and the outlays effects included in these estimates are detailed in Table 3.